An Introduction
to Christian Ministry

This book is dedicated
to
Olive, Martin, Stephen and Jonathan

An Introduction to Christian Ministry

Following Your Vocation
in the Church of England

GORDON W. KUHRT

CHURCH HOUSE
PUBLISHING

Church House Publishing
Church House
Great Smith Street
London
SW1P 3NZ

ISBN 0 7151 8111 4

Published 2000 by Church House Publishing

Cover design by Julian Smith

Printed in England by The Cromwell Press Ltd, Trowbridge, Wiltshire

Contents

Contents

Foreword

The Churches in England are changing. They are growing in ever closer partnership and becoming bolder in their prophetic witness to the nation. Among them the Church of England is changing in ways which are recognizable in every parish. No longer a bastion of a conservative establishment, it is accepting a missionary role in a nation which needs to hear the Christian message and to see it expressed in action at local, regional and national levels.

At the turn of the millennium a new prayer book is being launched which, while maintaining the ancient traditions of the universal Church, will bring a contemporary culture in touch with the worship in all parish churches. New central structures have brought a fresh sense of purpose and unity to the witness of the Established Church. Able theologians are contributing, from a Christian perspective, to the debates surrounding new ethical questions in the fields of global economics, gender, race and medical research.

Among these fresh opportunities, it is not surprising that new demands are being made of Christian ministry. Perhaps the most significant response over the last fifty years has been the emergence of lay ministry in many different forms. Lay Christians have taken new responsibilities in church government at both local and national levels. More lay people have become aware of the impact of the Christian faith, which can be made through their professional lives. Vocations have been taken up and skills have been honed to enable lay people to share in the liturgical, teaching and pastoral ministries of the Church.

What, then, of the ordained ministry? Thankfully, the exclusive nature of clericalism has declined but, alongside a healthy concept of ministry for all who are baptized, there is a pressing need to define the distinctiveness of the ordained ministry. It is not a distinction which describes ordination as bestowing superior gifts or which gives clergy the right to adopt a leadership role in all things. Yet the biblical roots of ministry and the accepted traditions of the Church do require an ordained ministry which has a singular vocation, which requires its own special preparation and training and which is confident of its role amidst all the tasks which the Church is called upon to fulfil.

In an ever changing social environment, and in a Church which is changing to meet new demands, the ordained person or the aspiring ordinand needs to be clear about what is required of him or her and how the Church will support them.

This book addresses these issues and, within the limitations of a short compass, provides the biblical and historical background to the ordained ministry as we see it today. It describes the qualities which are needed, the training which the church provides, and the tasks which are expected of the newly ordained.

Few people are better qualified to provide this new and timely review than Gordon Kuhrt. He has wide experience of many aspects of ordained ministry and, in his role as Director of the Ministry Division of the Archbishops' Council, is in a position to influence the shaping of the ordained ministry for the next generation.

I hope the book will be read by members of congregations who are on the look-out for ordinands among their number. I hope it will encourage clergy to take a new look at their own ministry in the light of both our heritage and our future. But most of all I hope it will inform many people who are considering their own vocation and give them courage in responding to it. The Church needs holy, thoughtful and imaginative people among its clergy. This book will help to discover them.

✠ Michael Dunelm:

Bishop of Durham and Chairman of the Ministry Division of the Archbishops' Council

Preface

There are many books on ministry issues and some are excellent. However, good *introductory* books are not readily available.[1] The writer is very conscious that in this volume many issues are not addressed, and that each of those which are could be dealt with far more profoundly.

I have not attempted an evenness of attention to the various topics. Extra space has been given to certain subjects which I regard either as particularly important in an Introduction or as matters which, I judge, receive insufficient attention elsewhere.

Much of the material has been the basis of numerous lectures, seminars, sermons and addresses in recent years throughout England and in Cardiff, Rome, and Uppsala. To all those of different churches with whom I have discussed these matters, I am most grateful. Aspects of the lecture or homiletic origin of parts of the material may still be discerned at various points.

I gladly acknowledge the stimulus of many colleagues, staff of the Ministry Division and those in the dioceses, colleges, courses and our various committees. I particularly thank the Chairman of the Division, the Bishop of Durham, the Revds Roy Screech, Mark Sowerby, Stephen Cottrell, Richard Burridge and Graham Cray, Hamish Bruce, Linda Foster and my secretary, Mary Ingledew. My wife and sons have given constant encouragement and critique.

Acknowledgements

The author and publisher gratefully acknowledge permission to reproduce copyright material in this book. Every effort has been made to trace and contact copyright holders. If there are any inadvertent omissions we apologize to those concerned and will ensure that a suitable acknowledgement is made at the next reprint.

Scripture quotations are taken from the HOLY BIBLE, NEW INTERNATIONAL VERSION Copyright © 1973, 1978, 1984 by International Bible Society. Used by permission of Hodder & Stoughton Ltd., a member of the Hodder Headline Plc Group. All rights reserved. NIV is a registered trademark of International Bible Society; UK trademark number 1448790.

Extracts from *The Alternative Service Book* 1980 are copyright © The Archbishops' Council of the Church of England and are reproduced by permission.

Extracts from *The Canons of the Church of England*, 5th edn, 1993, are copyright © The Archbishops' Council of the Church of England and are reproduced by permission.

'St Patrick's Breastplate' by Cecil F. Alexander, after St Patrick, is taken from *Hymns for Today's Church*, Hodder & Stoughton, 1982. Copyright © in this version Jubilate Hymns. Reproduced by permission of Hodder & Stoughton Ltd. (pp. 104-5).

Introduction

What is ministry? Do you want a very short answer or a rather longer answer? The short answer is that ministry is service to God and to others. Now while that answer is true, there are all sorts of other questions that come jumping out of it – and it is these questions that need rather longer answers.

Who are ministers? The ordained clergy, presumably, but what about lay ministers and ministry?

Where is ministry? In church, presumably, but what about ministry in the world?

How do people minister? By preaching, sacraments and pastoral care certainly, but what about all the other gifts and skills God gives people?

When do people minister? At worship, presumably, or when 'working for the church', but what about the rest of life? What does it mean to be 'in full-time ministry'? What is 'part-time ministry'?

All these – and many more – are fair questions. The evidence in the Bible is quite substantial and complex. The two thousand years of Christian history and the experience of many different churches or denominations around the world has often made the answers (and the questions) more complicated.

But let's start with some ordinary stories about a day in the life of –

1.   The Revd John Smith is vicar of Christ Church parish. It's Thursday. He prays and reads his Bible. He plans the church services for next Sunday, talks to the organist/music director about hymns and songs, and arranges people to read the Bible lessons and lead the prayers. He does some more work on a sermon. He writes some letters, makes and receives telephone calls and writes an article for the church magazine. He looks through the agenda for a committee meeting planned for the evening. At midday he has a funeral service at the crematorium. On the way home he visits a couple of folk in the hospital and another lonely person in her home. At 4.00 p.m. he has a weekly game of squash with a friend, and then from 5.30 – 6.30 p.m. he has a 'family-time' with the children home from school. Though John is vicar of a Church of England church and parish, his day is not untypical of a day for a 'full-time' minister/pastor/priest in a Methodist, United Reformed, Baptist or Roman Catholic church.

2.   The Revd Sheila Brown is a hospital chaplain. She was 'on call' last night, and was called out once to an emergency that involved a fatal accident, grieving families and young staff shaken by it all. During the day she systematically visits the wards and takes Holy Communion to those who have requested it. She plans the chapel mid-week service, works on a rota of volunteers from local churches, and talks to a young mother about a funeral service for her baby who died after only minutes of life.

3.   The Revd Jack Frost is ordained but is a school science teacher 'full-time'. He loves the work, the school, the young people and enjoys the friendship of colleagues. He had been a lay leader for many years in his church. When he was about forty, the vicar encouraged him to do the ordination training course. This did not involve going away to College but was a three-year course requiring one evening per week for lectures, several weekends away and an annual ten-day Summer School. Jack often helps the head teacher with leading assemblies at school. He has an occasional 'Christian Group' with a speaker and discussion and with the Religious Education teacher, organizes weekend 'house-parties' both for fun and for thinking about the deeper questions of life and faith. He helps the vicar by sometimes leading services, preaching every two or three weeks, and being a 'friend and colleague' with four lay people in the church 'ministry team'. He is single and lives with his widowed mother.

Now these three people are all ordained – but Sheila's main place of work is a hospital not a parish. Her work is sometimes called 'sector ministry'. There are ordained chaplains whose main place of work is an institution – hospital, college, prison or barracks. There are also 'sector' ministers who offer specialist skills in education, social issues, counselling or evangelism, etc.

Jack's main focus is as a science teacher and he has always seen that as service for God and his students. He does not artificially inject religious bits into his science lessons because he has always seen science as 'thinking God's thoughts after him'. His ordained ministry is 'non-stipendiary' (i.e. unpaid – although the church reimburses his 'working expenses'). His ordination has given him more of a 'representative' role in both school and church (this idea is discussed in Chapter 5) and an authority in speaking about God and Christian living.

But we need to hear some other stories from people who are *not* ordained –

4.	Anne White is 61 and has recently retired from a lifetime of work with senior responsibilities in a bank. Her husband died three years ago. She is an energetic woman and gives many hours every week to the Citizens' Advice Bureau, prison visiting, a Mums and Toddlers Group, running an Emmaus course and helping the vicar with all sorts of administrative tasks. Where, how and when is there ministry in Anne's work?

5.	Ian Webb has had two periods of unemployment and some acute depression but is now a hospital porter. Much of the work is humdrum but he tries very hard to be faithful and cheerful to anxious patients and stressed staff. He prays for people quietly in his mind. He listens to people and sometimes offers simple words of encouragement and faith in God. At church he is not into committees or teaching in Sunday School but he cuts the grass regularly and does many other practical jobs. He is a welcoming sidesman who will always spot newcomers and make sure they feel at home. What is the ministry in Ian's life?

It is difficult to see what isn't ministry in some way. Surely it isn't a matter of:

ordained	or	lay
church	or	world
paid	or	unpaid
worship	or	practical things
prayer	or	work.

The way in which these different categories overlap and intertwine may be seen from the chart overleaf:

	Church		World	
Ordained clergy	services	weddings funerals	visiting homes factories hospitals schools	family life/friends possibly 'secular' job hobbies/ recreation
	sermons	services/talks in hospitals and schools where many listeners never or rarely go to church		
Lay people	Sunday School home group committees preaching choir	open youth club bereavement group drop-in club practical work	Citizens' Advice Bureau prison visiting Parents – Teachers Association	family life 'secular' job hobbies/ recreation

but where do we put –

> evangelism;
> pastoral caring;
> prayer;
> Bible study?

So – what is ministry? It starts with Jesus.

1

Jesus – The Model

The ministry of Jesus is where we must start. Jesus said to his disciples:

> You know that those who are regarded as rulers of the Gentiles lord it over them, and their high officials exercise authority over them. [43]Not so with you. Instead, whoever wants to become great among you must be your servant [deacon or minister], [44]and whoever wants to be first must be slave of all. [45]For even the Son of Man did not come to be served [ministered to], but to serve [deacon, minister], and to give his life as a ransom for many.
>
> (Mark 10.42-45)

It is frequently said that all Christian ministry finds its source, its model and its authority in the ministry of Jesus. But it is easy to *say* this without really investigating what such assertions mean.

What did Jesus' contemporaries observe in his ministry? They saw a prophet who:

- preached to the crowds about the kingdom of God and often used different kinds of parables – some very short proverbs or aphorisms and also longer stories with a plot and several characters;

- taught the various groups of disciples – particularly about himself and his vocation;

- engaged in dialogue and controversy with the various groups who opposed him – including Pharisees, Sadducees and Herodians;

- offered God's reign, forgiveness and salvation especially to groups of people who were on the margins of society – religiously, socially and culturally – they included women, children, prostitutes, tax-collectors, foreigners;

- performed wonderful deeds which included healing the sick, liberating the demon-possessed and feeding the hungry;

- was persecuted and executed – this death was understood by Christians as 'for our sins' and 'according to the Scriptures' (1 Corinthians 15.3, and compare 'you are to give him the name Jesus, because he will save his people from their sins', Matthew 1.21);

- was raised to life on the third day – again 'according to the Scriptures' (1 Corinthians 15.4).

Jesus' life was one of service to God and to people: 'I am among you as one who serves' (Luke 22.27). This service/ministry had many facets. It is all too easy to select our favourite aspects of Jesus' ministry and ignore others.

However, in any consideration of Christian ministry we should note the explicit nature of his *example*. As the passage at the head of this chapter reminds us, Jesus supremely displayed the character not of 'lording it over others' but of 'serving others'. This characteristic does not mean that he did not have and display authority and power. The evidence is that he did exercise remarkable authority both in his teaching and in his mighty signs. Nevertheless, this authority was intimately and inextricably linked with a humility, a gentleness and an unselfish submission both to the will of the Father in heaven and the concerns of people on earth, especially the marginalized.

Frequently, in discussions on Christian ministry there is debate about the relative importance of who people *are* and of what people *do*, between being and doing (the technical words are ontology and function). But this distinction often becomes problematical and merely theoretical. In actual life, there is the closest of links between human being and human doing at its deepest levels.

This close connection is very evident in the ministry of Jesus. The character of his life was one of humble service, and that was the character of his active functions too. His practical ministry was dominated by two great areas of activity:

preaching and teaching;

caring – through miracles and counsel.

One of the most loved and evocative titles of Jesus is that of shepherd. No doubt it is often sentimentalized but it continues to speak (even to an urban society) of caring and costly ministry. It is a title with a lengthy Old Testament history but is specially applied to Jesus in the Fourth Gospel: 'I am the good shepherd. The good shepherd lays down his life for the sheep' (John 10.11).

2

Frequently ministry is virtually identified with the pastoral (shepherding) ministry. We need to remind ourselves that this included feeding (teaching) and searching for the lost (evangelism).

These activities were conducted with a serving attitude, both to God and to others. There was a perfect blend of the being and the doing. Humility and authority, service and power were united in a seamless robe.

I shall resist the temptation to develop this rich seam of thought. Jesus is also described as:

the apostle	Hebrews 3.1
the deacon	Romans 15.8
the overseer (*episcopos*)	1 Peter 2.25
the priest	Hebrews 5.6
the teacher	Matthew 23.10
the minister in the sanctuary (*leitourgos*)	Hebrews 8.2.

There are many good books about Jesus. The four Gospels and studies of the life of Jesus will be a continual resource for reflection and inspiration for Christian ministry in our times.[1]

What is the relation between the ministry of Jesus as described in the Gospels and the ministry of God's people today? It appears that there are both similarities/continuities and differences/discontinuities.

Similarities and continuities

Sent by God;
witness to God's kingdom by preaching, teaching and signs;
ministering to human need through care and healing;
servant-like in attitude;
filled with God's Spirit.

These features are all characteristic of the ministry of Jesus and they should be characteristic of the service of Christian people today. The Fourth Gospel writer tells of the risen Jesus saying to the disciples 'As the Father has sent me, I am sending you' (John 20.21). Jesus 'went throughout Galilee, teaching in their synagogues, preaching the good news of the kingdom, and healing every disease and sickness among the people' and sent his disciples to preach, teach, care and heal too (Matthew 4.23; cf. Luke 9.1-6; 10.1-20;

Matthew.28.18-20, etc.). Jesus washed the disciples' feet, and said 'Now that I, your Lord and Teacher, have washed your feet, you also should wash one another's feet. I have set you an example that you should do as I have done for you' (John 13.1-17). Jesus came to serve and give his life and he calls his disciples to be like him (Mark 10.42-45 quoted at the beginning of this chapter). Jesus' ministry was constantly in the power of the Holy Spirit (Luke 3.22; 4.1,14,18, etc.) and he promises the same Spirit and power to his disciples (Luke 24.49; John 20.22; Acts 1.8, etc.).

These similarities or parallels are significant and striking. From one point of view the relationship is not surprising. The teaching of Jesus expounded in the Fourth Gospel laid the foundation for a strong tradition in later Christian theology of a most intimate relationship between Jesus and his followers. There are the strange words attributed to Jesus in the 'John tradition' to amplify his assertion 'I am the bread of life'. He added, 'unless you eat the flesh of the Son of Man and drink his blood, you have no life in you . . . those who eat my flesh and drink my blood remain in me, and I in them' (John 6, especially verses 53 and 56). Again 'All who have faith in me will do what I have been doing' (John 14.12). Again 'I will not leave you as orphans; I will come to you . . . I am in my Father, and you are in me, and I am in you . . . Those who love me will obey my teaching. My Father will love them, and we will come to them and make our home with them.' (John 14.18,20,23).

Paul too has a strong theology of the Christian's unity with Christ. It starts with baptism into Christ and thus into his death and into his resurrection (Romans 6.1-5). The phrase 'in Christ' is a regular feature in Pauline writing. In the last analysis, he puts everything to one side 'that I may gain Christ and be found in him . . . I want to know Christ, and the power of his resurrection and the fellowship [*koinonia*, partnership] of sharing in his sufferings, becoming like him in his death, and so, somehow, to attain to the resurrection from the dead' (Philippians 3.8-11). Paul's understanding of Christian ministry is not only to be a 'minister *of* Christ Jesus' but he also affirms, 'I glory *in* Christ Jesus in my service to God. I will not venture to speak of anything except what Christ has accomplished through me in leading the Gentiles to obey God by what I have said and done – by the power of signs and miracles, through the power of the Spirit' (Romans 15.17-19; author's emphasis).

Nevertheless, we must be cautious. In spite of these most significant similarities, and the strong theologies of union with Christ, we must also note any differences and discontinuities.

Differences and discontinuities

There is an utter uniqueness about Jesus Christ which must not be forgotten
or diminished. Failure to recognize this uniqueness could lead to a distorted
application of some of the features just considered. There was/is a uniqueness in:

- Jesus' nature as Son of God, Son of Man, Messiah and Lord;

- Jesus' authority:

  in his teaching: 'Truly, truly I say . . .'; 'You have heard it
  said, but I [emphatic in the Greek] say . . .';

  in his signs and mighty works in nature, in healing and over
  evil spirits;

- Jesus' death (not as martyr but) as atoning sacrifice for sin;

- Jesus' priesthood and heavenly intercession – see Hebrews 7 – 10
  (especially 7.24,25).

This uniqueness of Jesus' nature, authority, atoning death and resurrection
means that we must be cautious about drawing straight lines of similarity or
continuity between the earthly ministry of Jesus and the ministry of Christians
today.

As Christians reflect on his role as *source* of Christian ministry, as *model* for
ministry and as the *authority* for it, they will remember not only that Christians
are called to be *in* Christ and to participate in aspects of the ministry of
Christ, but also that they are paradoxically followers and disciples *of*
Christ. Sometimes the disciples follow at a distance (as famously did Peter, cf.
Matthew 26.58), sometimes they fail in understanding, obedience and
holiness. Because of this human (and sinful) frailty, Christians must be very
cautious about claiming a corporate (let alone an individual) continuity with
the ministry of Christ. His ministry was perfect because of his total faithfulness to the Father and the vocation of the people of God. Christian ministry
today is similar to, and continuous with, the ministry of Jesus Christ only to
the degree that it too is faithful to the Father and the vocation of the people
of God.

But like the Israel of the biblical period and the Early Church, individual
Christians and Christian churches today are frail. They are often weak both in
understanding and holiness. We fail to love God with all our mind, heart, and
strength. Here is a fundamental difference.[2]

However, there is another 'difference' which is startling. In the Fourth Gospel, Jesus is reported as saying 'I tell you the truth, anyone who has faith in me will do what I have been doing.' This seems to speak clearly enough of the continuity between Christ's ministry and that of his followers. However, he goes on 'They will do *even greater things* than these, because I am going to the Father' (John 14.12; author's emphasis). How can Christians do 'greater things' than Jesus' powerful preaching and powerful signs? The classic answer has been that the coming of the Holy Spirit has enabled the teaching and works of Jesus to spread with remarkable rapidity *first through* Western Asia, then into Europe, to Rome and beyond . . . and eventually to the ends of the earth. The expansion of the mission in terms of human conversions and impact on the world is of an extraordinarily different order to the relatively small-scale ministry of Jesus in first-century Palestine. This is a quite different kind of discontinuity.

The ministry of Jesus is of vital significance as we consider the ministry of Christ's Church. In spite of all the frailties and failures of the Church's life. He is:

its *source*	—	for he calls his people to ministry;
its *model*	—	for he is the example of ministry;

and:

its *authority*	—	for he commissions and empowers through his Spirit.

There are discontinuities because of the utter uniqueness of Christ, but we must, nevertheless, keep looking to Jesus, the great Shepherd of the sheep (Hebrews 12.2 and 13.20).

2

Church and Ministry

Our thinking about ministry requires an understanding of God's calling to the *whole* Church. For too long ministry has been thought of as the preserve of the clergy, the ordained ministers. One frequently hears it said of someone at a theological college that she (or he) is 'preparing for the ministry' or 'going into the ministry'. But the early Christians did not talk like that, and we need to look carefully at the New Testament to see how they thought about and practised ministry. There are four key ideas that are vital for thinking about the whole Church and ministry.

The people of God

An important Greek word is *laos*. From this word, of course, we get the word laity, and immediately we can be plunged into confusion. The word *laos*, people (of God) is used in different ways, and it is very important for us to be clear about the way we are using it.

It is used of the people of God. Thus it is used of Israel, and it is used of the whole Church. In 1 Peter 2.9-10 we read: 'You are a chosen people, a royal priesthood, a holy nation, a people [*laos*] belonging to God, that you may declare the praises of him who called you out of darkness into his wonderful light. Once you were not a people [*laos*], but now you are the people [*laos*] of God.' The language here used of the followers of Jesus, the early Christians, is clearly taken from the Old Testament language used of Israel, the covenant people of God.

But secondly (and this is where the confusion starts) *laos* could be used to describe *ordinary* folk (as opposed to leaders and experts). Now we can use it in that way in modern English. People are heard to say in the course of a discussion about the law or medical matters, 'of course, I'm only a layman in this area', and they mean they are not specially skilled, experts, or professional. So, in Bible times, the word *laos* was sometimes used of the 'ordinary' Israelites who were not priests (the religious professionals).

Then, thirdly, the word came to be used in the Church for those who were not clergy. This development is not in the New Testament. It began about AD 200 when first the bishops and later the presbyters (elders) gradually came to be called priests. (We shall look at this particular issue in the next section below).

But the meaning of *laos* as the whole people of God is the primary meaning in theology and thinking about the Church (ecclesiology). When used in this primary and fundamental way, the clergy are part of the laity – the ordained people are part of the whole people of God. Often, the secondary usages of the word (the unskilled or the unordained) have obliterated the primary meaning, and so distorted views of the church and ministry. Even when people know this in the head they find it difficult to live by it – the distance from the head to the heart has been called 'the longest journey in the world'. In the Church of England's levels of government, elections and sometimes voting are divided into the 'House of Clergy' and 'House of Laity'. This again misleads many into thinking this usage is primary, when actually it is secondary.[1]

The priesthood

The Greek word is *hierateuma* which comes from *hiereus*, a priest. In English we have the words hieratic (priestly) and hierarchy (government through graded ranks or priesthood). In the New Testament the word 'priest' is never used of clergy or church leaders. It is used of those responsible for worship in Old Testament Israel (e.g. Hebrews 9.6) and other traditions (e.g. Melchizedek of Salem, Hebrews 7.1). It is also used of Jesus – especially in the letter to Hebrews, e.g. 'Fix your thoughts on Jesus, the apostle and high priest whom we confess' (3.1).

The word priesthood is also used of the whole people of God, the whole church – 'you are a chosen people, a royal *priesthood*, a holy nation, a people belonging to God . . .' (1 Peter 2.9; author's emphasis). It is also worth noting Revelation 1.5b-6 'To him who loves us and has freed us from our sins by his blood, and has made us to be a kingdom and *priests* to serve his God and Father – to him be glory and power for ever!' (and 5.10 similarly; author's emphasis).

It was later in the second century that the words priest and priesthood came to be used specifically first of bishops and then of presbyters. This was strongly developed in the third century. The development seems to have come about through analogy with those responsible for worship in Old Testament Israel. At this time, the Greek *hiereus* is translated into the Latin *sacerdos* (from which we derive the English word sacerdotal – meaning priestly). In the Middle Ages, and widely in Roman Catholic and Eastern Orthodox Churches today the title and order of priest expresses the sacrificing role of the ordained minister in the Eucharist or service of Holy Communion. It is argued that the Jewish priest had an essential role in the offering of sacrifice at the altar in the tabernacle or Temple, and similarly, presbyteral clergy today have an essential role in the offering of sacrifice at the Lord's table, the Christian altar. The Protestant Reformers (especially Martin Luther, John Calvin and, in England, Archbishop of Canterbury Thomas Cranmer) were very critical of aspects of this argument and argued strongly for a reformed understanding which (as they saw it) would return more closely to a New Testament understanding. They particularly emphasized the priest-hood of the whole people of God (an emphasis which had certainly become much obscured in the Middle Ages). It is important to note that the sixteenth-century Reformers did not speak primarily about all Christians being individual priests, but that all Christians are *corporately* sharing in the priest-hood of the whole people of God.

Now, although the English Reformers shared this 'Reformed' theology of ordained ministry, they retained the word priest in the *Book of Common Prayer*. This has led to some confusion. Archbishop Cranmer and many of his colleagues were highly educated, and, though committed to reform (much of it quite radical), were also careful to maintain continuity wherever that was appropriate. They argued that the word 'priest' in English did not necessarily have the connotations deriving from the Latin *sacerdos* (with its explicitly sacrificing emphasis) but was a legitimate contraction of the title presbyter (often translated into English as 'elder'). This argument is extensively devel-oped in the later sixteenth century by major scholars such as Bishop Jewel, 1522–71, Archbishop Whitgift, 1530–1604, and the eminent theologian Richard Hooker, 1554–1600.[2] This usage in the *Book of Common Prayer* also made it clear that deacons were not to celebrate Holy Communion.

Now whatever the strengths and weaknesses of the argument about a particular priesthood of the clergy (sometimes called ministerial priesthood – considered again in Chapter 5) we must remember that the primary New Testament teaching about priesthood is about either Jesus Christ himself or about the whole Church of Jesus – and *not* about the clergy or ordained leaders.

Ministry

The main Greek word often translated 'ministry' is *diakonia*. The word also means 'service'. A *diakonos* is a servant.[3] From these words we get the English words deacon and diaconal. Once again, these words are used in different ways and we need to disentangle the different layers.

Firstly, ministry (*diakonia*) is used for all God's people. They are expected to exercise ministry/service through the spiritual gifts (see pp. 11–13) given to them by the ascended Christ. After a reference to hospitality in verse 9, we read in 1 Peter 4.10: 'Each of you should use whatever gift you have received to serve [the verb from *diakonia*] others, faithfully administering God's grace in its various forms.' Now, as we shall see shortly, all God's people are given 'gifts of the Spirit', so all are called to use these gifts in service/ministry towards God and others.

But, secondly, the word came increasingly to be used of those in leadership or ordained ministry. We noted at the beginning of this chapter the way in which people often talk of those preparing for ordination as 'going into the ministry'. This language has been common not only in the churches of catholic traditions but also of the reformed traditions.

Thirdly, in some church traditions (e.g. the Baptists) a deacon is a lay person who is appointed or elected to assist in the leadership of administrative tasks of church business. However, the group of deacons have often taken on considerable pastoral roles in collaboration with, or in the absence of, a pastor (often called 'the minister').

Other church traditions have sought to maintain the 'threefold order of ministry of the catholic tradition' – bishop, priest/presbyter and deacon (see further in Chapter 5). This usage of the word 'deacon' is complicated and will be discussed later (see p.53f.).

What we need to emphasize at this stage is that the primary meaning of ministry in the New Testament Early Church is of the service/ministry of the whole people of God. The other meanings are derivative and, in various ways, confusing for the fundamental point. As Emil Brunner puts it:

> One thing is supremely important; that *all* minister, and that nowhere is to be perceived a separation or even merely a distinction between those who do and those who do not minister, between the active and the passive members of the body, between those who give and those who receive. There exists in the *Ecclesia* a universal duty and right of

service, a universal readiness to serve, and at the same time the greatest possible differentiation of functions.[4]

The Ordinal in the Church of England's *Alternative Service Book* gets it absolutely right when (p. 351) in the first prayer by the bishop at the ordination service for priests/presbyters, he says

> Hear our prayer for your faithful people that each in their vocation and *ministry* may be an instrument of your love.

This prayer is for all God's people, and it is in this context that *some* are called to a particular ordained ministry.

Spiritual gifts

The New Testament Greek word for the gifts of the Holy Spirit is *charismata*. These are given to all God's people by the risen Christ, through the Holy Spirit and for the building up of God's Church and service to others. The New Testament evidence is:

> Romans 12.6: 'We have different gifts [*charismata*], according to the grace given us';

> 1 Peter 4.10: 'Each of you should use whatever gift [*charisma*] he has received to serve others, faithfully administering God's grace [*charis*] in its various forms';

> 1 Corinthians 12.4-7: 'There are different kinds of gifts [*charismata*], but the same Spirit. There are different kinds of service [*diakonia*], but the same Lord. There are different kinds of working, but the same God works all of them in everyone. Now to each one the manifestation of the Spirit is given for the common good';

> And in verse 11: 'All these [i.e. wisdom, knowledge, faith, healing, miraculous powers, prophecy, distinguishing spirits, speaking in tongues, interpretation] are the work of one and the same Spirit, and he gives them to each one, just as he determines.'

> See also Ephesians 4.7, 11-13.

There are four lists of spiritual gifts in the New Testament as follows:

Romans 12.6-8	1 Corinthians 12.8-10	1 Corinthians 12.28-30	Ephesians 4.11
prophesying	wisdom	apostles	apostles
serving	knowledge	prophets	prophets
teaching	faith	teachers	evangelists
encouraging	healing	workers of miracles	pastors
contributing to needy	miraculous powers	healing	teachers
leadership	prophecy	helping	
showing mercy	distinguishing spirits	administration	
	speaking in tongues	speaking in tongues	
	interpretation of tongues	interpretation	

None of those lists appears to be systematic or exhaustive. However, some of the gifts might be termed *leadership*-type gifts – apostles, teachers, pastors and leadership itself. We shall return to this matter of leadership in Chapter 4. Then there is a group of gifts that are sometimes called *supernatural*-type gifts – speaking in tongues, interpretation of tongues, working of miracles and healing. The designation 'supernatural' for this group is inadequate. Neither is it appropriate that some call these particular gifts 'charismatic' gifts. All the gifts are gifts of the Holy Spirit and have a 'beyond the natural' (supernatural) dimension.

Thirdly, there is a group of gifts that one is tempted to call *ordinary*-type gifts – helping, encouraging, administration, serving, showing mercy and contributing (money) for those in need. But this designation of 'ordinary' is inadequate too. Can a gift of the Holy Spirit of God really be ordinary?

What a modern world view calls 'natural' (or 'ordinary') and 'supernatural' seem to be mixed up in the lists of the New Testament. All spiritual gifts need to be understood as the initiative of the Holy Spirit through our humanity, sometimes bringing the foretaste of the powers of the age to come, and sometimes bringing a renewed touch of God to the creation abilities that he has already given.

Three further comments need to be made about spiritual gifts. Firstly, over the centuries, the clergy (the ordained ministers) have sucked too many of these *charismata* into the pastor-model, the presbyter-model or the priest-model. They have developed (and been allowed by the 'laity' to develop) almost a monopoly of most of the gifts mentioned. Secondly, the supernatural-type (sometimes called charismatic) gifts have been denied as real or appropriate in post-apostolic times by different forms of dispensationalism. They have, therefore, often been channelled off into either Pentecostalism or forms of the charismatic movement. Many of these gifts are now being acknowledged and welcomed into other theological traditions and the life of other churches. My third comment is that too often the so-called ordinary gifts have not been recognized as spiritual gifts at all. The result is that many lay people (using 'lay' in its secondary sense) have not been conscious that they are gifted by the Spirit in a particular and personal way and have been exercising such gifts when they have been helping, showing kindness and encouragement and performing numerous aspects of administration and giving money in the collection or offertory.

There have been confusions and misunderstandings about all four of these key ideas – the people of God, priesthood, ministry and spiritual gifts. As a result there has been through many centuries a *clericalism* that has magnified ordained ministry at the expense of lay ministry, and a *sacerdotalism* that has magnified the ordained priesthood at the expense of the priesthood of the whole people of God. The leadership *charismata* have been magnified at the expense of other *charismata* that may appear much more ordinary. So, was it an accident, or was it deliberate when the member of a congregation who was leading the prayers in the Litany of the *Book of Common Prayer* and, instead of saying *'illuminate* all bishops, priests and deacons' actually said *'eliminate* all bishops, priests and deacons'?

Ministry is the calling of all God's people. They are the royal priesthood, gifted by the Spirit for service to God and to their fellow human beings.

As I have shared this material in many lectures and seminars in theological colleges and courses, in cathedral lectures and diocesan clergy conferences, it has sometimes been heard as if it was new or radical. However, it is neither. There is nothing controversial in this understanding of the New Testament evidence – though it may be that it is rarely set out clearly or worked through coherently. The famous ecumenical report *Baptism, Eucharist and Ministry*[5] addresses each of these four issues in its 'Ministry' section.

3

Discipleship for All

The following chapters will increasingly focus on leadership of different kinds, and on the ordained ministry. But, before we do so, we must devote another full chapter to the ministry and priesthood of the whole people of God. Indeed, even when we do focus on leadership and ordination, it is vital that we continually keep the larger context in view and do not fall back into clericalism or sacerdotalism. The theological and spiritual reasons for this are uppermost, but there is a very practical reason too. Those of us who are responsible, in various ways, for selecting people for ordination training are sometimes criticized about the quality of clergy in the Church today. We are tempted to reply 'There is one big problem with the business of choosing new clergy – we only have the laity to choose from!' There is a saying 'We get the leaders we deserve!' The higher the levels of discipleship and spirituality among God's people generally, the higher the quality of the clergy is likely to be. Prayerfulness, expectations and encouragement will play their part.

There are three issues we can usefully consider here under the heading of the discipleship of the whole people of God – baptism, worship and mission:

baptism	–	the foundation
worship	–	the experience
mission	–	the consequence

Baptism – the foundation of discipleship[1]
The New Testament writers claim that human life is lived in one or other of two realms which are in dramatic and vivid contrast. We may be members of the old creation or the new creation, either in Adam or in Christ, in darkness or in light, living according to the sinful nature or by the Spirit, in death or in life, belonging to the world or belonging to God. These contrasts will be found in 2 Corinthians 5.17; 1 Corinthians 15.22; Ephesians 5.8 (cf. Colossians 1.13); Romans 8.5f.; 1 John 3.14 (cf. John 10.10); John 17.6-19. However, although the

conversion from one realm to the other is critical, and theologically a contrast that cannot be exaggerated, nevertheless from the human point of view that conversion may be a long, gradual and almost imperceptible process rather than a single, dramatic event. The New Testament writers nowhere require a sudden conversion experience, but do require convertedness – 'Unless you change [literally 'turn'] and become like little children, you will never enter the kingdom of heaven' (Matthew 18.3). Conversion means to turn around, to face the right direction, to be following Christ. The significant issue is not *when* or *how* but *whether* a person is going in the right direction, i.e. is converted (Acts 3.19; 26.18). The metaphor of 'being born again' (John 3) is more to do with the decisively new character of life with God than with the suddenness of its arrival in human experience.

Baptism is, by its very nature, a single definite event, but the human experience of conversion is not always (or even often) like that. Hence the relationship in time between baptism (the outward sign) and conversion (the spiritual reality) is not always a simple, obvious and straightforward one.

It is widely agreed today that baptism is the 'ordination of the laity', that is, God's commissioning of his people to ministry and service in the world. The entire gospel of God's redeeming *grace* is expressed in baptism. The promises and blessings of baptism are, of course, vitally related to *faith* in Jesus Christ. They include:

- Forgiveness and cleansing – 'Repent and be baptized . . . for the forgiveness of your sins' (Acts 2.38). 'Be baptized and wash your sins away' (Acts 22.16; see also 1 Corinthians 6.11; Ephesians 5.26; Hebrews 10.22; Titus 3.5).

- Belonging to and being identified with Christ – baptism is frequently described as 'in [into, Greek *eis*] the name of Jesus Christ' (Acts 2.38; Romans 6.3).

- Sharing in the death and resurrection of Jesus Christ – 'baptized into his death . . . buried with him through baptism into death . . . united with him . . . in his death . . . united with him in his resurrection' (Romans 6.3,4; Colossians 2.12).

- The gift of the Holy Spirit – Peter said 'Repent and be baptized . . . and you will receive the gift of the Holy Spirit' implying that water-baptism symbolizes Spirit-baptism. The pouring of the water dramatizes the outpouring of the Spirit (Acts 2.38; 1.5; Titus 3.5). This gift is a seal, a deposit, a guarantee assuring the inheritance of God's people until the final day of redemption (2 Corinthians 1.21f.; Ephesians 4.30; 1.13f.). This baptism is the mark both of present experience and a future hope, a realized indwelling and an anticipated consummation.

- New birth to adoption and sonship – 'He saved us through the washing of rebirth.' 'Children of God through faith . . . for all of you who were baptized into Christ have clothed yourselves with Christ' (Titus 3.5f.; Galatians 3.26f. and possibly John 3.5).

- Membership of the body of Christ – 'We were all baptized by one Spirit into one body' (1 Corinthians 12.13). This body is God's covenant community, his Church. Baptism marks initiation into the Church, the Christian fellowship.

It is clear that in the New Testament the word of the gospel and the sign of baptism are seen as a unity, and the same effects are attributed to both without contradiction or difference of meaning. The Presbyterian James Denney rightly said 'Baptism and faith are but the outside and the inside of the same thing',[2] and the Roman Catholic Rudolf Schnackenburg wrote 'Baptism without faith in Christ is unimaginable for the thinking of the primitive church.'[3] It is not that faith makes human beings worthy of such blessings, or that baptism has an intrinsic power to produce them; it is God who enables faith and gives baptism – and all the blessings are his alone. The blessings are only secondarily baptism-blessings or faith-blessings; primarily they are God's blessings. The Baptist George Beasley-Murray neatly says 'Baptism is the divinely appointed rendezvous of grace for faith.'[4] The New Testament theology of baptism and faith presupposes the missionary context and the administration of baptism to converts.

In the light of this emphasis on evangelism and faith, it is inevitable that baptism of converts will involve a confession of faith. However, it is intriguing that the New Testament writers nowhere indicate the significance of the baptism event in terms of the convert's witness to others. Rather it is God's witness or seal to the convert. The baptized *life* is seen as a witness to others rather than the baptism event.

The New Testament writers used baptism as a basis for, or illustration of, an appeal for holiness of life or the unity of God's people.

With respect to holiness, see Romans 6.3,4:

All of us who were baptized into Christ Jesus were baptized into his death. We were therefore buried with him through baptism into death in order that, just as Christ was raised from the dead through the glory of the Father, we too may live a new life.

With respect to unity, see 1 Corinthians 12.13 in the context of an appeal for unity in Christ:

For we were all baptized by one Spirit into one body – whether Jews or Greeks, slave or free – and we were all given the one Spirit to drink.

and Galatians 3.26-29:

You are all children of God through faith in Christ Jesus, for all of you who were baptized into Christ have clothed yourselves with Christ. There is neither Jew nor Greek, slave nor free, male nor female, for you are all one in Christ Jesus. If you belong to Christ, then you are Abraham's seed, and heirs according to the promise.

Baptism is not simply a sign of God's saving action in the *past* (in Jesus' death, resurrection and gift of the Spirit) or God's saving action in the *present* (in the application of that eternal covenant plan to an individual's experience through regeneration and conversion), but also God's saving action in the *future* (in the Spirit's outworking of fruit of character and gifts of service, and pledge of final redemption). The Christian is summoned to live a baptismal life. Because s/he is baptized, say the apostolic writers, the Christian must live a pure life, realize Christ living within, put to death the old life and live out a resurrection life, live according to the Holy Spirit, as a child of God, a member of Christ's body. Having been initiated, the convert is called to live accordingly. Become what you are – baptized, believer, set apart for God, recipient of the covenant promise.

Baptism is a ceremony, but a ceremony that provides a pattern and shape for the whole of Christian life. It is not so much a single service or event, more a way of life. The truth of baptism as an event will only be understood when the reality of baptism as a way of life is lived and experienced.

The World Council of Churches Faith and Order Commission Paper[5] speaks of the high significance of baptism for the practical life of the Church. It says:

[S]ince baptism encompasses the whole Christian life, lack of clarity concerning the meaning of baptism leads to uncertainty all along the line. It is beyond dispute that in no church body does baptism have the decisive significance which the witness of the New Testament ascribes to it. Here we all have much to learn. A serious penetration into the meaning of baptism and an appropriation of the treasure given in baptism would give *preaching* and *teaching* both a centrally focused content and a new breadth, together with an insight which clarifies and unifies the whole of christian life. The more the baptised learn to see their whole life in the light of their baptism, the more does their life take on the pattern of life 'in Christ'.

The baptism event provides a pattern and shape for the baptized life. The baptized life is the life of Christ, life in and through Christ, Christian life, a converted life. Just as the marriage ceremony is a decisive event but must then be worked out through married life, so too baptism is a decisive event but must be worked out through Christian life. Just as the marriage ceremony marks the beginning of a new way of life, so too with baptism. Baptism is for living.

1.   *Baptism enshrines encouragement* and unequivocally focuses the life of discipleship of Jesus Christ. The divine blessings symbolized in and offered through baptism are entirely offered in and through Jesus Christ. The gift of baptism understood as covenant sign reminds the believer of the priority and initiative of God's grace, of the faithfulness of God's covenant promise through the ages, and of the incredible costliness of God's salvation in Christ. As in the other sacrament ordained by Christ, the Lord's Supper, there is no greater encouragement than to be turned back to Christ as the centre, the focus and the determining factor of life. Christian people need constantly reminding that in baptism they are forgiven and cleansed, they belong to and are identified with Jesus, they share in the significance of his death and resurrection, they receive the gifts of the Holy Spirit, they are adopted as children of God and become members of the Body of Christ, the Church. These blessings are not automatic or unconditional but are offered through the gospel to those who receive that good news by faith. Here is great encouragement for the believer. But there is a second point.

2.   *Baptism clarifies commitment* for its blessings in Christ clearly imply discipleship to Christ. The blessings *from* him will not be enjoyed unless there is continuing faith *in* him and submission to him. The baptized life is a Christ-centred and Christ-empowered life – apart from him we can do nothing.

The multiple significance of baptism gives a definite shape to the Christian's commitment. Having been cleansed and forgiven, there must be a continuing concern for holiness and purity of life. Having been identified with Jesus Christ, there must be a continuing submission to him, and life through him.

Having participated in his death and resurrection, there must be a continuing putting to death the deeds of the sinful nature and a continuing setting of the mind on resurrection life. Having been baptized with the Spirit, there must be a continuing walking by the Spirit, being filled with the Spirit, showing the fruit of the Spirit and using properly gifts of the Spirit. Having been born again into God's family, there must be a continuing life of acknowledging God as *Abba*, Father, and developing the family likeness. Having been baptized into the Body of Christ, the Church, there must be a continuing life of Christian fellowship, inter-dependence and service. Thus baptism expresses the dimensions of all that God offers, and, at the same time, clarifies the nature of the appropriate response.

It cannot be over-emphasized that God's blessings are neither automatic nor unconditional. Thus baptism must only be understood, offered and received in the context of the gospel of Jesus, received by faith and issuing in a life of discipleship. Christian life is a baptism-shaped life, and Christian ethics are 'baptism ethics'.

Infant baptism makes theological sense in the context of the believing family and the Church. The baptized infant grows up as a believer within that faith-context. It is when the significance of a living faith or the implications of baptism are reduced that great problems develop both of theology and of pastoral practice.

Baptism is no more mere theoretical theology than it is mere ceremonial rite – it is profoundly practical, and relevant to the individual life of the Christian and corporate life of the Church. Just as there are no blessings in Christ which are not symbolized in baptism, there are no aspects of discipleship and obedience that are not implied by or consequent upon baptism.

Augustine thought of baptism as like a soldier's badge or uniform. It is, he said, the same sign which both identifies the soldier and convicts the deserter. Baptism then enshrines all the encouragement of God's covenant promises but it also reinforces all the responsibilities of God's covenant requirements.

Like a wedding ring, baptism joyfully reminds the Christian of the love and commitment *of* the one who gives it. It also reminds of the obligation of faithfulness *to* that one who 'loved me and gave himself for me'.

Worship – the experience of discipleship

Paul writes in Romans 12.1-12:

> Therefore, I urge you, brothers and sisters, in view of God's mercy, to offer your bodies as living sacrifices, holy and pleasing to God – this is your spiritual act of worship. [2]Do not conform any longer to the pattern of this world, but be transformed by the renewing of your mind. Then you will be able to test and approve what God's will is – his good, pleasing and perfect will.
>
> [3]For by the grace given me I say to every one of you: Do not think of yourself more highly than you ought, but rather think of yourself with sober judgement, in accordance with the measure of faith God has given you. [4]Just as each of us has one body with many members, and these members do not all have the same function, [5]so in Christ we who are many form one body, and each member belongs to all the others. [6]We have different gifts, according to the grace given us. If your gift is prophesying, then use it in proportion to your faith. [7]If it is serving, then serve; if it is teaching, then teach; [8]if it is encouraging then encourage; if it is contributing to the needs of others, then give generously; if it is leadership, then govern diligently; if it is showing mercy, then do it cheerfully.
>
> [9]Love must be sincere. Hate what is evil; cling to what is good. [10]Be devoted to one another with mutual affection. Honour one another above yourselves. [11]Never be lacking in zeal, but keep your spiritual fervour, serving the Lord. [12]Be joyful in hope, patient in affliction, faithful in prayer.

This passage begins with a great 'Therefore'. Because of God's mercy shown to us in Christ incarnate, suffering, crucified, but now risen and exalted, and shown in the gift and work of the Holy Spirit . . . therefore! We have seen how God's mercy is expressed and sealed in baptism . . . therefore! The consequence of following the Suffering Servant is that his disciples will be worshipping people. Here is the call to all God's people to a total, wholehearted discipleship marked by sacrificial worship.

This will be worked out in daily experience in four ways:

Your bodies – offered (v.1)

The offering of sacrifices was an integral part of the regulations for worship in early Israel. They might include the life of animals and birds or the gift of grain or wine. Sacrifice was a category of worship understood throughout the ancient world.

Christians are here urged not to offer money or possessions but their very lives as a living sacrifice to God. The 'body' means the whole of life. God is not concerned merely with what is sometimes described as the 'soul', or the 'spiritual' side of life, or our attendance at church worship. He is concerned with, and expects to be, Lord of every part of life. 'Do you not know that your bodies are temples of the Holy Spirit, who is in you, whom you have received from God? You are not your own; you were bought at a price. Therefore honour God with your bodies' (1 Corinthians 6.19, 20).

It is discipleship in working life – in banking, industry, commerce, law, education, government, media, entertainment; it is discipleship in the local community, in the family and amongst neighbours; it is discipleship in national affairs and international responsibility; it is discipleship in justice and the stewardship of earth's resources – all this, as well as discipleship in prayer, sacraments and 'church life'.[6]

Some aspects of such daily, living sacrifice are clear. It will be costly – for it is utterly comprehensive and excludes no aspect of life, relationships or possessions. It is to be holy and pleasing to God – that is, the sacrifice is to be made according to *God's* standards rather than our own. God's standards are so uncomfortably and uncompromisingly totalitarian – 'Love the Lord your God with all your heart and with all your soul and with all your mind' and 'Love your neighbour as yourself' (Matthew 22.37-39 and parallels, quoting Deuteronomy 6.5 and Leviticus 19.18).

Finally, it is this living sacrifice which truly is 'spiritual worship' (or 'reasonable service' in some translations). Worship/service is not confined to 'church' worship or services; it encompasses every aspect of life.

Your minds – transformed (vv.2-3)

Very frequently, it is the way we *think* that determines the way we speak and the way we act. If we do not *think* that truth is sacred and important, it is likely we shall give into the temptation to lie. If we do not *think* that people of all ethnic origins and colours are equally created in the image of God, and equally the objects of his love, it is likely we shall succumb to the temptation of racism which speaks of others, and acts towards them, as inferiors. The mind matters!

Paul says, 'Do not let your mind be squeezed into the mould of *this world*.' He is using 'this world' as a way of describing society which ignores God and his law, his will, his word and his love. God made the world, loves the world and is at work in the world through his Spirit, but this world in general has turned away from God, and rejected Jesus Christ as Saviour and Lord. So, rather than following the thought-patterns of this world and the spirit of this age, we need a transformation through the mind being converted and renewed.

The Great Commandment (quoted in the previous section) says that we should love God with all the *mind*. How is our mind to be renewed? Quite simply – by accepting the Triune God as our Teacher. We must be disciples of God's Word, of Jesus' teaching and of the Holy Spirit's illumination. Paul says, 'But we have the mind of Christ' (1 Corinthians 2.16), and then 'Your attitude should be the same as that of Christ Jesus' (Philippians 2.5). An intellectual and moral conversion is part of discipleship. The Church is to be a learning organization – hearing God's word, thinking through its implications, and then working them out in all aspects of daily life.

This is why the dimension of preaching and teaching is so important for Christian leadership and the ordained ministry of the Church. This is developed in Chapter 4 (p. 33ff.).

The call to a life of holy sacrifice or of sacrificial holiness requires that we use our minds 'to test and approve what God's will is'. This exacting and demanding task must be applied to justice issues in the world, to moral issues in the individual, to evangelism and apologetic in the community, and to the edification (building up) of the Church.

Your gifts – used (vv.3-8)

It is vital that Christians are not conceited in this area (v.3), but make a sober and realistic appraisal of the way they should be serving God – both in community and church life. None of us has all the gifts or skills or knowledge – no one is omnicompetent.

In verse 4 Paul develops his famous metaphor of the body with its many parts which all have different tasks and responsibilities. It is to be like this for those who are 'in Christ', that is, God's people. However, while avoiding conceit and the temptation to exaggerate our importance, we must recognize that each of us is given gifts, ministries, tasks and so must fulfil our responsibilities in family, the wider world and in the church's life. In verses 6 to 8 Paul gives some examples of how gifts are to be used. We are to serve God and others with enthusiasm and commitment, with diligence and with cheerfulness.

Jesus told parables about people being entrusted with responsibility in God's kingdom (the talents, Matthew 25 and the pounds, Luke 19). The thrust of these parables seems to be that when we use our gifts properly they may be multiplied or developed. On the other hand, if we decline to use them, we may lose them!

Your character – genuine (vv.9ff.)

The final part of Romans chapter 12 moves again towards issues of inner motivation and character. We have seen how the sacrificial service of our daily lives requires a mind that is taught by God. Now we find that if gifts are to be used properly they must express a character that is taught by God.

Paul gives a series of exhortations. They begin with 'Love must be sincere.' The word sincere means genuine, the same all the way through, with no hypocrisy, no pretence. Love is fundamental to Christian discipleship. The Law of God is summarized as love for God and love for neighbour. Love is the fulfilling of the Law of God. Without the warm generosity of love, law obser- vance can degenerate into a dry and rigid legalism or an external and almost unfeeling following of duty. God so *loved* the world that he sent his Son to be the Saviour. Paul ends his famous hymn of love by saying, 'And now these three remain: faith, hope and love. But the greatest of these is love.' (1 Corinthians 13:13). The life offered in sacrifice, the mind conformed to the will of God, gifts used with commitment for the kingdom of God – all these need to be motivated, warmed and energized by the love of God 'poured into our hearts by the Holy Spirit' (Romans 5.5).

When these foundations are in place, then the remarkable and challenging exhortations to further aspects of discipleship continue –

- hate what is evil; cling to what is good;
- be devoted to one another in brotherly/sisterly love;
- honour one another above yourselves;
- never be lacking in zeal, but keep your spiritual fervour, serving the Lord;
- be joyful in hope;
- patient in affliction;
- faithful in prayer;

23

- share with God's people who are in need;

- practise hospitality;

- bless those who persecute you;

- rejoice with those who rejoice;

- mourn with those who mourn;

- live in harmony with one another;

- do not be proud, but be willing to associate with people of low position;

- do not be conceited, etc., etc.

Here is a vocation to all God's people to a discipleship which reaches into every aspect of life with a summons to complete commitment to God and his kingdom. The idea that a vocation to ordained ministry is a *'higher* calling' is very difficult to sustain in the light of the biblical understanding of both baptism and worship.

Mission – the consequence of discipleship

'The Church exists by mission as a fire exists by burning' is a famous saying. If baptism is the ordination to Christian discipleship, and if sacrificial worship and holiness is the lifestyle of discipleship, then mission will be the inevitable consequence. Mission is not an optional extra for Christians who are interested in that sort of thing; it is not an extra dimension to be bolted on. It is of the essence of discipleship for all God's people.

Mission is ultimately God's mission. The word *missio* means 'sending'. In creation, God sends his Spirit and his Word. In redemption, God sends his Son and his Spirit again. 'God so loved that he gave his one and only Son . . .'. Jesus said, 'As the Father has *sent* me, I am *sending* you' (John 3.16; 20.21; author's emphasis;). Jesus said, 'I am going to send you what my Father has promised . . .' (Luke 24.49).

The whole world, and human beings within it, are in a state of profound disorder. The created order is subjected to frustration . . . the whole creation has been groaning . . . it, and we, are longing for redemption, salvation, liberation and a righteous order (Romans 8.20-27). The Bible uses many metaphors to express this disorder. A particularly significant description for the plight of human beings is lostness. In Luke 15, we find Jesus' parables of the lost sheep (and searching shepherd), the lost coin (and searching woman), the lost son – or was it sons? – (and the waiting and pleading father). An inadequate appreciation of the radical disorder in human nature and its consequences will inevitably result in an inadequate grasp of the missionary mandate. The dimensions of mission include evangelism, but also much more.

Mission is to the world. Mission seeks to meet the concerns in the Lord's prayer:

> hallowed be your name,
> your kingdom [reign] come,
> your will be done
> on earth as it is in heaven.
>
> (Matthew 6.9-10)

These concerns cover every aspect of life and creation. Thus, sharing in the mission, the concerns, the activity of God will include:

- the stewardship of God's created order and especially of earth's resources;

- the service of others through every kind of pastoral care and social responsibility;

- the sharing of the good news of Jesus Christ (evangelism);

- persuading people of its truth and relevance (apologetic);

- the pursuing of justice and peace for all.

The so-called Great Commission is often misquoted, and thereby reduced in its immense breadth. Jesus is reported as saying ' . . . go and make disciples of all nations . . . teaching them to obey everything I have commanded' (Matthew 28.19-20). Thus, the vocation of God's people is to multiply disciples, and the vocation of disciples is to engage in the whole mission of God.

Who is sufficient for these things? No one – but whenever God calls, he also empowers. Thus he sends his Holy Spirit upon Jesus at his baptism, the beginning of his public ministry, and upon the disciples for their ministry and witness. This empowering work of the Holy Spirit in and for mission is a major motif of the two volumes of Luke, the Gospel and the Acts of the Apostles (and/or of the Holy Spirit).

Too often mission is seen as the enthusiasm of the few rather than the responsibility, privilege and vocation of all God's people. This privilege and responsibility includes both the evangelistic and the social justice dimensions of mission. Of course, some are particularly 'gifted' in evangelism and/or called to be evangelists. Others have a particular passion for issues of justice, peace and social concern. However, that does not reduce the impact of the expectation that all God's people are called to be witnesses to the love and kingdom of God, to the forgiveness and justice of God, to God's offer of new life and salvation in all its aspects.

The starting point of mission for all of us is where we are – our family, friends, neighbours and communities of relationships. With many of these people we will share ties of language, culture and interests. However, God's mission does not stop there. It traverses boundaries, crosses cultures and involves new languages. The incarnation of Jesus Christ and his ministry in Palestine was a supreme cross-cultural leap. Then, he went out of his way to meet with, give dignity to and share the kingdom of God with those on the margins – and beyond. He taught women in public, gave dignity to children, mixed with prostitutes, tax-collectors and Samaritans and touched those with leprosy.

The account of the early missions and Church growth in Luke's second volume highlights the cultural, language and geographical boundaries that are crossed and challenged – from Judaea to Samaria, to Syria, to Asia Minor, to Greece, to Rome and beyond. Thus the apostolic nature of the Church essentially includes both the apostolic message (its content) and the apostolic mission (its strategy). The word apostle is from the Greek word meaning 'to send' and similar to the Latin origin of mission and missionary. Thus, all members of the people of God are called to be witnesses for God's mission where they *are*, but also alert to the possibility that God might be calling them to *go* somewhere else and *do* something else.

The traditional (especially nineteenth- and early-twentieth-century) understanding of missionary work was about relocating to another country, usually far away. It still can mean that, but it could also mean getting involved in communities very close or within your own country which have significantly different language or style of language, culture(s) and concerns.[7]

In this chapter, we have seen how:

> *baptism* involves the vocation of all God's people to a baptized
>   life of discipleship;
> *worship* is the vocation to holy living of all God's people in
>   every aspect and relationship of daily life;
> *mission* is the inevitable outworking of that life of discipleship
>   and will be as extensive as the concerns of God himself.

4

Leadership

We have seen in Chapter 2 that ministry in the New Testament is a very large concept. It is not used simply of those who are ordained let alone of a professional elite group of leaders. We saw that the whole people of God (the *laos*) are the priesthood, and all are called to ministry (*diakonia*) in their daily lives – that is, service to God and to others. Furthermore, we found that God gives the gifts of his Spirit to all his people in order to equip and energize them for this service in many different kinds of ways.

In Chapter 3 we further explored some of the radical implications of discipleship and of God's mission for all of his people.

All this has been (and still is) frequently misunderstood among Christians. So often clericalism of different kinds has magnified ordained ministries at the expense of lay ministries. So often sacerdotalism has magnified the ordained priesthood at the expense of the priesthood of the whole people of God.

This history and experience is an important part of the reasoning in Christian groups which reject the idea of ordination and clergy altogether. The Christian Brethren and the Society of Friends are examples. During the last three decades of the twentieth century there has been a dramatic development of consensus among all the Christian churches on the ministry of the *whole* people of God (see Chapter 2) and that this is foundational to all further developments of ministry.

Nevertheless, there are particular kinds of ministries, gifts and titles in the New Testament which indicate very clearly (and at the very least) roles of leadership of different kinds. These are spoken about in many contexts, in many different ways. However, there seems to be a developing clarity and emphasis about both their roles and their qualities and qualifications.

The reality of leadership

There are very ambivalent attitudes to leadership in both the Church and the world today. On the one hand, there are constant appeals for good, strong, wise and visionary leadership at all levels. And yet, on the other hand, there is widespread suspicion of, and even cynicism about, leadership.

The New Testament is very clear that among the gifts given to and ministries exercised by all God's people, there are particular gifts and ministries of leadership. Different words are used and will now be listed. However, the translation of these words is fraught with difficulty. This may be due to the way in which a word has become associated with historical controversy, or the way in which the same word has been translated or developed in quite different ways by different churches or theological traditions. Some of the main words are:

- *apostolos* – apostle, literally someone who is *sent* (with authority). Jesus himself is called by this title (Hebrews 3.1). He called the twelve apostles (Matthew 10.2) who parallel the twelve patriarchs of Israel. The title was also used regularly by Paul (e.g. Galatians 1.1), and occasionally of others, e.g. Barnabas (Acts 14.14). It probably came to mean missionary or church-planter.

- *presbyteros* – presbyter, often translated as elder. The early Christian churches in Palestine seem to have organized their leadership to resemble the Jewish synagogue's board of elders in Jerusalem (Acts 11.30;15.22). Paul and Barnabas followed this example on their missionary journey – they 'appointed elders for them in each church'(Acts 14.23). See also Titus 1.5.

- *episcopos* – literally overseer, but could be translated superintendent. It is commonly known in English as bishop (through Anglo-Saxon corruption of the Latin *episcopus*). They were clearly church leaders at Philippi (Philippians 1.1). It is widely agreed that in the earliest days *presbyteros* and *episcopos* were interchangeable (see Acts 20.17, 28). However, in the early second century, the bishop became the president of the presbyters.

- *diakonos* – deacon, literally servant or minister. We have already seen that Jesus' ministry was diaconal (servant-like), and that all God's people are called to serve him and others (p. 10). However, the word came to be used in a special way of a particular kind of function or office. It is traditionally associated with the appointment of the seven men in

Acts 6.1-6 who were given responsibility to administer the charitable distribution of aid to poor widows, although the noun *diakonos* is not used in the story. However, it clearly occurs later (Philippians 1.1 and 1 Timothy 3.8) referring to a particular kind of leader. Phoebe was a woman deacon (Romans 16.1). In recent years, the scholar John Collins has questioned the traditional understanding of this word. He has argued that it conveys a strong element of the 'go-between' and thus spokesperson, courier and agent. It is, he argues, a word equally applicable to positions of authority and dignity as to those of low esteem.[1]

Other leadership-type names or functions might include prophets, teachers, evangelists, pastors (see the lists of spiritual gifts in Chapter 2, p. 12). The lists of gifts in Romans 12 includes the general word leadership – if a person's gift 'is leadership, then govern diligently' (vv. 6,8).

The Greek word used here prompts us to look at four other passages where general leadership words are used:

● Remember your *leaders*, who spoke the word of God to you. Consider the outcome of their way of life and imitate their faith. (Hebrews 13.7)

● Obey your *leaders* and submit to their authority. They keep watch over you as those who must give an account. Obey them so that their work will be a joy, not a burden, for that would be of no advantage to you. (Hebrews 13.17)

● Now we ask you brothers and sisters to respect those who work hard among you, who *are over you* in the Lord and who admonish you. Hold them in the highest regard in love because of their work. (1 Thessalonians 5.12, 13a)

● The elders who *direct the affairs* of the church well are worthy of double honour, especially those whose work is preaching and teaching. (1 Timothy 5.17)

In the first two passages from the letter to the Hebrews, the word used is *hegoumenos* which can be translated ruler, governor or leader. In the following two quotations the verb *proistemi* is again used (as in Romans 12.8) which means to rule, direct, manage or superintend.[2]

Finally, there are the shepherding words that lead to the designation pastor (Ephesians 4.11). Especially important is 1 Peter 5.2-4 because it relates the church pastors to Jesus Christ himself – 'Be shepherds of God's flock that is under your care, serving as overseers (*episcopoi*) . . . And when the Chief

Shepherd appears, you will receive the crown of glory that will never fade away.' Also in Acts 20.28 Paul urges the overseers (*episcopoi*) of Ephesus to 'keep watch over . . . the flock . . . be shepherds of the church of God, which he bought with his own blood.'

Here are ministries of leadership which are explicitly gifts of the Holy Spirit. Here are functions or offices to which the Holy Spirit appoints (Acts 20.28), and/or the apostles, other church leaders or the church community. If it is disastrous (as it is) when clericalism magnifies ordained ministries at the expense of the ministry of the whole people of God, it is also disastrous when the Church does not recognize and truly value these ministries of leadership. This is because the supreme responsibility of church leadership is to *enable* the Church to be what God calls her to be. This leads us to consider the responsibilities of leadership.

The responsibilities of leadership

It is clear that in the earliest churches there was no single or systematic pattern of leadership. The church at Corinth had many serious problems of division, immorality and confusion over worship, doctrine and behaviour, yet Paul never appeals to the leaders in this particular church. This may be because the leaders were very much part of the problems – the factions in the church were associated with the names of leaders such as Paul, Apollos, Cephas (Peter) or even Christ himself (1 Corinthians 1.12). Or it may be because the leadership in this church was very fluid or charismatic – that is, leaders emerged in various situations and were authenticated by the spiritual gifts they demonstrated at the time (see 1 Corinthians 11-14).

An overarching principle of leadership in the New Testament is clearly demonstrated in Mark 10.35-45. James and John asked Jesus if they could have special places of honour next to him. Jesus points them in the direction of sharing his suffering rather than his glory – 'You will drink the cup I drink and be baptized with the baptism I am baptized with.' When the other disciples are indignant, Jesus reminds them that the way of the world is for rulers and officials to *lord* over others. But 'not so with you. Instead, whoever wants to become great among you must be your *servant* [deacon], and whoever wants to be first must be *slave* of all. For even the Son of Man [Jesus himself] did not come to be served but to serve . . .' (author's emphasis)

Nevertheless, leadership of different kinds is vital to the health and well-being of God's Church. So we read in 1 Timothy 3.1 'Here is a trustworthy saying: If anyone sets his heart on being an overseer (*episcopos*), he desires a noble task.' Also we note Paul's exhortation to the Corinthians, 'Follow the way of love and eagerly desire spiritual gifts especially the gift of prophecy' (1 Corinthians 14.1, see also v.39).

Three responsibilities seem to be particularly emphasized:

To *be an example*

'Remember your leaders . . . Consider the outcome of their way of life and *imitate* their faith' (Hebrews 13.7; author's emphasis). 'Be shepherds . . . over-seers . . . not greedy for money, but eager to serve, not lording it over those entrusted to you, but being *examples* to the flock' (1 Peter 5.2,3; author's emphasis). 'Set an *example* for the believers in speech, in life, in love, in faith and in purity' (1 Timothy 4.12; author's emphasis).

This constitutes a real problem for many people today. In many parts of the world, perhaps particularly in Western countries, there is a strongly egalitarian current in the culture.

Ideas of example and imitation may smack of an outmoded view of deference. However, we often speak of the importance of role-models for young people, and of mentors who not only advise by word of mouth but model a way of life.

The Church of England Bishops' report *Issues in Human Sexuality*[3] was criticized for having 'double standards' – a stricter one for clergy and another for lay people. Actually it sought to clarify the biblical teaching of sexual morality for all God's people alike. Then when it came to practical issues of church life today, it did argue that church leaders have a particular responsibility to be an exam-ple. The Report says:

> From the time of the New Testament onwards it has been expected of those appointed to the ministry of authority in the Church that they shall not only preach but also live the Gospel. These expectations are as real today as ever they were. People not only inside the Church but outside it believe rightly that in the way of life of an ordained minister they ought to be able to see a pattern which the Church commends . . . the example of its ordained ministers is of crucial significance.[4]

> On the question of the clergy as role models, the Ordinal of 1662 and the Canon Law do indeed require those ordained deacon and priest to make both themselves and their families wholesome examples and patterns to the flock of Christ.[5]

Much recent writing on ordained ministry emphasizes the priority of *being* over *doing*. Sometimes this is all rather vague. However, where the content of the being is about holiness of character and a Christ-likeness of example then it is, undoubtedly, an absolute priority.

It is a weighty responsibility for church leaders to be an example, a model, a pattern. But it is clearly both biblical, and practical and realistic. Whether we like it or not, the leader's life will be closely observed, and 'actions speak louder than words'.

To exercise pastoral care

'Obey your leaders and submit to their authority. They *keep watch* over you . . .' (Hebrews 13.17; author's emphasis). The New English Bible has 'they are tireless in their concern'. It is surely in this context that we should understand the reference to 'those who are over you in the Lord and who *admonish* you' (1 Thessalonians 5.12; author's emphasis). The word 'admonish' can be translated 'counsel' (as in the New English Bible). The word *episcopos* literally means someone who oversees, watches over. The early Christian communities took pastoral care very seriously. They followed the example of Jesus who had a special concern for the afflicted, the oppressed and the needy. An early controversy for the Christian church in Jerusalem arose over the pastoral care of and provision for widows. There was a feeling that the Greek-speaking Jews were not being given equal treatment with the Hebraic Jews. The apostles regarded the issue of great importance. Although they knew it should not distract them from their personal priorities of preaching and prayer, they proposed the appointment of high calibre men 'full of the Spirit and of wisdom' to oversee the diaconal tasks. These men were commissioned with prayer and the laying on of hands (Acts 6.1-6).

The early Christians certainly looked eagerly for the return of Christ and the final completion of God's kingdom. But they were not so heavenly minded as to be of no earthly use. Paul was particularly committed to the early 'Christian aid' project of the collection of money for the poverty-stricken Christians in Jerusalem (see 1 Corinthians 16.1-4 and 2 Corinthians 8 – 9).

Paul's letters are largely sustained and careful exercises of pastoral care for the churches. Good teaching is an essential part of such care and we shall consider that shortly. The theological and doctrinal teaching in the letters continuously interweaves with ethical and practical guidance – it is always theological ethics and theological spirituality. A proper understanding of freedom in Christ will lead to life in the Spirit and the fruit of holiness (Galatians

5 – 6). A thorough appreciation of the spiritual blessings of new life in Christ will lead to a commitment to unity in the Body of Christ, living as children of the light, and practical implications for daily relationships of wives and husbands, children and parents, and slaves and masters (Ephesians 5 – 6).

Similar outlines of Christian teaching and its practical implications for daily life will be found in other letters of Paul, Peter and John. This is pastoral care and counsel of the highest order. The letters to the seven churches of Asia Minor in Revelation 2 – 3 are cameo examples of that passionate care for the churches that fully reflects the compassionate (and even perplexed) concern of Jesus for his disciples during his earthly ministry. The letters speak of God, they often congratulate, they warn of dangers and they offer hope, forgiveness and renewal of life in Christ. They are 'the Spirit speaking to the churches' – theological, pastoral, passionate and practical.

To *preach and to teach*

'The elders who direct the affairs of the church well are worthy of double honour, especially those whose work is preaching and teaching' (1 Timothy 5.17). The New Testament leaves us in no doubt about the importance of preaching and teaching. It was important for Jesus. In his own ministry he preached powerfully, persistently and imaginatively to the crowds. He taught patiently and privately to individuals (e.g. Nicodemus and the Samaritan woman, John 3 and 4) and to his disciples. He engaged in repeated debates of controversy with the Jewish leaders. He sent his disciples on preaching missions, and before his ascension to heaven the parting commission was 'Go and make disciples of all nations, baptizing them in the name of the Father and of the Son and of the Holy Spirit, and teaching them to obey everything I have commanded you' (Matthew 28.19-20).

The Acts of the Apostles shows us how they obeyed Jesus. Luke gives us examples of a few of the outstanding sermons of Peter and Paul in different contexts. He repeatedly emphasizes the spiritual power and persuasiveness of the preaching and the consequent dynamic growth and expansion of the infant Christian groups.

The Pastoral Letters to Timothy and Titus consist of advice to Christian leaders and their church communities about the pattern and priorities of their life and ministry. From 1 Timothy – false teaching is disastrous (chapter 1), the overseer must be 'able to teach' (3.2), 'command and teach these things . . . devote yourself to the public reading of Scripture, to preaching and to teaching' (4.11,13). From 2 Timothy – 'keep as the pattern of sound teaching' (1.13), 'the things you have heard me say in the presence of many witnesses entrust to reliable people who will also be qualified to teach others . . . Do your best to present yourself to God as one approved, a worker who does not need to be ashamed and who correctly handles the word of truth . . . able to teach . . . gently instruct' (2.2,15,24,25) 'from infancy you have known the holy Scriptures, which are able to make you wise for salvation through faith in Christ Jesus. All Scripture is God-breathed and is useful for teaching, rebuking, correcting and training in righteousness, so that God's servant may be thoroughly equipped for every good work' (3.15-17); 'Preach the Word; be prepared in season and out of season; correct, rebuke and encourage – with great patience and careful instruction' (4.2). And finally from Titus – an elder 'must hold firmly to the trustworthy message as it has been taught, so that he can encourage others by sound doctrine and refute those who oppose it' (1.9); 'You must teach what is in accord with sound doctrine . . . In your teaching show integrity, seriousness and soundness of speech that cannot be condemned' (2.1,7,8).

Why was there such a repeated emphasis on these matters in the Pastoral Epistles? – presumably because they were regarded as so critical for the life and health of the churches. Why have I risked the tedium of quoting all these passages? – because I believe that many church leaders today and their Christian communities do not realize sufficiently the health-giving qualities of the Word of God rightly taught and thoughtfully applied into the contemporary situation. Many do not appreciate the gravity and danger of a situation where there is an unrecognized famine of the Word of God with its consequent under-nourishment, spiritual weakness, and vulnerability to infections which can result in terminal decline and death.

I have more stories about preaching in my card index than about any other single subject. Some of them are amusing and will provoke laughter – but like much humour, there is a sad and serious, even deadly edge.

There is the story of the vicar's daughter, sitting next to her mother in the vicarage pew, whispering 'why does daddy say that short prayer before the sermon?' Her mother replied, 'To ask for God's help in preaching.' 'Why does not God answer his prayer then?' Or there is another story of the pastor, who at the beginning of his sermon, apologized for the sticking plaster on his face and said 'While I was shaving this morning I was thinking about my sermon and cut my face.' Someone handed him a note at the door 'Why don't you think about your face and cut your sermon?'

Some suggest that denigration of preaching is because times have changed. It is culturally incredible that one should simply quote from letters from the first century. So we turn to the second half of the twentieth century. John Stott, in his book I *Believe in Preaching* gives many modern stories.[6]

One of the greatest theologians of our century, Karl Barth, said:

> It is simply a truism that there is nothing more important, more urgent, more helpful, more redemptive, more salutary, there is nothing from the viewpoint of heaven and earth, more relevant to the real situation than the speaking and the hearing of the word of God in its originative, and regulative power of truth.[7]

The Roman Catholic Second Vatican Council (1962–5) said about the exploration and exposition of the Divine Writings:

> This task should be done in such a way that as many ministers of the Divine Word as possible will be able effectively to provide the nourishment of the scriptures for the people of God thereby enlightening their minds, strengthening their wills, and setting people's hearts on fire with the love of God.[8]

Archbishop Michael Ramsey in *The Christian Priest Today* asks 'Why the Priest?' He answers the question:

> First the priest is the teacher and preacher and as such the man (sic) of theology. He is pledged to be a dedicated student of theology and his study need not be vast in extent but it will be deep in its integrity, not in order that he may be erudite but in order that he may be simple. It is those whose studies are shallow who are confused and confusing.[9]

Over many years I have worked for the College of Preachers. Sometimes people gently mock and say; 'Why do you give time to preaching. How many people remember sermons?' To which I gladly reply; 'How many meals can you remember. It doesn't mean to say that they haven't done you any good. You can only remember a few outstanding meals in your life – special anniversaries, parties, weddings. But in actual fact it is that steady diet of ordinary food, day in, day out, over the years which has made you what you are.' And that is what the preaching/teaching ministry is. It is not basically meant to be spectacular. There are few spectacular sermons but most of them are ordinary fare that build people up and help them become servants of God, out in the world in their daily lives as well as serving in the Church.

We have spent quite some time on the *importance* of preaching and teaching, but now more briefly we consider the *character* of this responsibility. There are two metaphors used in the New Testament that shed light on what preaching/teaching is about.[10]

The first one is the *steward* (in Greek *oikonomos*). The classic passage is 1 Corinthians 4.1-2: 'So then, you ought to regard us as servants [deacons] of Christ and as those entrusted [stewards] with the secret things of God. Now it is required that those who have been given a trust must prove faithful.' Stewards in biblical times were people with great responsibility and authority. What greater responsibility, authority and privilege than to be entrusted with (steward of) the good news from almighty God through Jesus Christ and in the power of the Spirit, and the care of the churches.

The second metaphor about the character of preaching and teaching is the *herald* (in Greek *keryx*). Paul says, 'We preach [herald] Christ crucified . . . the power of God and the wisdom of God . . . God was pleased through the foolishness of what was preached [the *kerygma*, the message of the herald] to save those who believe' (1 Corinthians 1.23, 21). A similar metaphor is that of *ambassador*. 'We are therefore Christ's ambassadors, as though God were making his appeal through us. We implore you on Christ's behalf: Be reconciled to God' (2 Corinthians 5.20). The herald and the ambassador are people with great responsibility and authority. They represent a sovereign or a government. What greater responsibility, authority – yes, and privilege – than to announce news from the King of Kings, and, on his behalf (exercising a gift granted through his Spirit) to have a care of the churches. Like Jesus – proclaiming and appealing. In preaching and Christian teaching there should be an authority and boldness – but also a winsome appeal, a gentle instruction.

We can, thirdly, consider the *method* of preaching and teaching. The second half of the twentieth century has seen a charismatic renewal through many Christian churches with its greater emphasis on the experienced work, gifts and power of the Holy Spirit in individual Christians and in the Church corporately. There has been much enthusiasm about charismatic theology of tongues, of healing and of prophecy. Not so much attention has been accorded to charismatic theology of preaching. An outline will be found in 1 Corinthians 2 – in four stages:

- God *reveals* the gospel by his Spirit (v.10) because no one knows the thoughts of God except the Spirit of God (v.11).

- We *understand* that revelation that God has freely given us only through the Spirit we have received from God (v.12).

- The human *preacher speaks* not with human wisdom but in words taught by the Spirit, expressing spiritual truths in spiritual words (v.13).

- This preaching can only be *received* through the Holy Spirit for those without the Spirit do not accept the things that come from the Spirit of God. For they are foolishness to them and they cannot understand them because they are spiritually discerned. So in this way 'we have the mind of Christ' (vv.14-16).

We need teaching about preaching, preaching about teaching, sermons about what sermons are about. We need to recognize and explain that preaching is a dialogue even when people in the congregation do not literally talk back. Preaching is an encounter with the living God that demands response. If the listener is spiritually attentive there will be a growth of spiritual sensitivity; if the listener is careless there can be a spiritual hardening. Here is an aspect of eternal drama.

Not only is the preacher to be in the Spirit and giving the words of the Spirit, but the audience, the congregation, must be in the Spirit, listening and receiving through the Spirit and even being discriminating by the Spirit. Hence Karl Barth spoke about expectancy: 'When the Church bell rings there is in the air an expectancy that something great, crucial, even momentous is to happen. What is it? It is the people's expectation that they will hear God's Word, that is answers to their ultimate questions.'[11]

It is the charismatic conviction of the sovereign role of the Holy Spirit in the revelation of God's gospel and in the illumination of human hearts and minds that underlies the requirement that preaching is not only through the Spirit but also according to the Word. Thus, the ministry of Jesus was 'in order that the Scripture might be fulfilled'. Thus, the risen Jesus Christ on the road to Emmaus with the two disciples 'explained to them what was said in all the Scriptures concerning himself' (Luke 24.27). Thus, the very early creed found in 1 Corinthians 15.3,4 reiterates the point:

Christ died for our sins according to the Scriptures;

he was buried;

he was raised on the third day according to the Scriptures.

What was the *content* of the preaching and teaching? What was so important? What was entrusted to the steward and proclaimed by the herald and ambassador? What was revealed by the Spirit in Scripture, and illumined by the Spirit in the heart?

Paul summed up his preaching as 'the gospel of God's grace' (Acts 20.24 and 32). One of the fears of some Christian leaders is of not knowing what to preach or of 'running dry'; criticisms of congregations are that some preachers have little passion and teach their own ideas rather than the Word of God. If the gospel of God's grace does not stir the blood, fire the heart and excite the mind; if there is no urgent desire to share this gospel and explore all its consequences, then there is a spiritual illness or depression which needs urgent and immediate attention (see Chapter 9).

More particularly, the gospel of God's grace is focused in the *death and resurrection of Jesus Christ*. Peter says, 'You . . . put him to death . . . but God raised him' (Acts 2.23-24). Paul speaks of 'the message of the cross . . . the power of God . . . we preach Christ crucified . . . the power of God and the wisdom of God . . . I proclaimed to you the testimony about God . . . Jesus Christ and him crucified . . . with a demonstration of the Spirit's power' (1 Corinthians 1.18,23f.; 2.1-5).

This gospel has a very large context in the *kingdom* (the reign) of God which comes in a new and decisive way in the life, teaching, miracles, death and resurrection of Jesus Christ. So Jesus came 'preaching the good news of the kingdom' (Matthew 4.23). Paul, too, gave himself to 'preaching the kingdom' (Acts 20.25). Is our preaching as big, as wide, as eternal and yet as applied, as is implied by the reign and rule of Christ breaking into our world, our community, our home, our work, our private thoughts and ambitions?

So Paul was able to say to the Ephesian elders 'I have not hesitated to proclaim to you the whole will of God' (Acts 20.27). The 'simple gospel' of God's love has endless consequences for every aspect of life. Thus the *kerygma*, the proclamation of good news moves into the *didaché*, the teaching. That is why no hard line can be drawn between evangelism and nurture; that is why the evangelist and the pastor/teacher must work together at every stage.

This draws us, finally, to one of the great *objectives* of the teaching ministry – that is, to equip and enable God's people for their own ministries in daily life (cf. Chapters 2 and 3). This equipping role is a combination of teaching and pastoring. It is described classically in Ephesians 4.11-13: 'It was he [Christ] who gave some to be apostles, some to be prophets, some to be evangelists, and some to be pastors and teachers, to prepare God's people[12] for works of service, so that the body of Christ may be built up until we all reach unity in the faith and in the knowledge of the Son of God and become mature, attaining to the whole measure of the fulness of Christ.'

To be effective in this area, leaders need to know their people and understand something of both their personal/family and working/business lives and contexts. Visiting homes and places of employment is very important. Also required is a heart-concern for their spiritual maturing. This concern will be seen in intercession. Michael Ramsey's famous description of such prayer is evocative – 'to be with God with your people on your heart'.[13]

Again and again throughout history and across the world this kind of preaching and teaching has warmed hearts, converted lives, instructed minds, corrected behaviour, changed community attitudes, challenged monarchs and governments. Is that surprising when people truly believe it is the power and the wisdom of God?

There, then, are the three major responsibilities of Christian leaders set out repeatedly in the New Testament writings:

> example;
>
> pastoral care;
>
> preaching and teaching.

The Ordinal (service of Ordination) in the Church of England *Alternative Service Book* picks up all these themes in a very effective way. It speaks about ' proclaiming the Lord' in the declaration, 'calling hearers to repentance', 'being an example' 'ministering to the sick', 'caring for the people, teaching and admonishing'. It talks about 'growing up into the likeness of Jesus Christ'. In the questions, the interrogation of the ordinand – 'Will you expound and teach the Scripture? Will you fashion your own life and those of your house-hold according to the way of Christ? Will you make Christ known to all people?' And then later, in the actual laying on of hands – 'Will you watch over them? Will you care for them? Will you proclaim the good news of salvation?'

Here is a high calling indeed! Is anyone sufficient for these things? We shall turn now to the character and qualifications of Christian leadership, but let us delay a moment longer. We have noted that the leaders' example is to be imitated. We have seen that the leaders' authority (note the plural leaders throughout the passages quoted on page 29) is to be obeyed. However an insensitive and autocratic authoritarianism (often by a single leader) is deeply flawed and destructive. The authority of the leaders is not their own, it is the authority of the Word and the Spirit of God – to be received with discrimination and spiritual sensitivity by their sisters and brothers in Christ. The leaders' work is to be respected (see 1 Thessalonians 5.13 and 1 Timothy 5.17 quoted on page 29). 'Hold them in the highest regard in love because of their work' – the Greek word is a *triple* intensive translated by the New English Bible – 'hold them in the highest possible esteem and affection.' It is almost embarrassing. How can we keep a balance between avoiding an improper adulation and yet giving and receiving genuine heartfelt esteem and affection? Some clergy, pastors and other Christian leaders do not discover how much people love them and owe to them until the day they leave a particular church or appointment. Of course it needs to be mutual – leaders who love much will probably be greatly loved.

The character of leadership

The writers of the books that came to be called the New Testament were deeply concerned about leadership, and the quality and qualities of their church leaders. The early churches had plenty of problems in this area – false apostles, prophets and teachers, division and antagonism, problems of immorality, greed and pride. Some of these issues will be specifically addressed in Chapter 9.

The general character of Christian leadership has been indicated earlier in the chapter at page 31 as the servant (diaconal) nature of the Lord Jesus himself – humble service to God and to others.

Aspects of the character of leadership are implicit in the responsibilities expounded above – the leader will have a spirituality and lifestyle which is exemplary, will exercise pastoral care and counsel that is both compassionate and wise, will preach and teach with authority and humility that comes from submission both to the Spirit and the Word of the living God. But surely, we must object, you cannot and should not expect any single person to have all these gifts and qualities – the omnicompetent minister either does not exist, or is heading for a breakdown, or is a stopper in the bottle preventing the flowering and exercise of the spiritual gifts of others. True! However, although the Christian leader may not be outstanding in both pastoral care and preaching/teaching, she or he should at least be competent in these two areas. This is not *omni*-competence. There are plenty of other areas of spiritual giftings in which the Christian leader may have little or no contribution to make, e.g. specialist evangelism and church planting, administration, healing, miracles, practical helping, speaking in tongues and interpretation. In a contemporary church situation, the leaders may look to many others to edit and produce the church magazine, manage the finances, organize the committees, lead work among children and young people and do much detailed work with evangelistic groups, pastoral visiting and care for property, etc.

In the passages on leadership quoted on page 29 there are clear restraints on the leaders. They are accountable to God, will have to answer to him for every aspect of their stewardship. They will be expected to work hard (not *too* hard, for we will look at this issue more closely later; see page 100ff). It will be hard work to live an exemplary life and to be a caring pastor and effective preacher. Then leaders are 'over you *in the Lord*'. There is a common identity of all Christians including their leaders which comes from believing in the Lord, being baptized into Christ, and so living a life which is 'in Christ our Lord'. Leaders are called to be over others but not superior to them. This is not a moral, religious or spiritual superiority – but it is leadership!

There is much more that could be said on this topic. I am tempted to undertake a systematic overview or summary, and that would have its place and usefulness. In Chapter 8 I quote the Church of England's published summary of criteria for selection of people to train for ordination. However, instead of that approach, on this occasion I invite you to look at passages of the New Testament which deal with the topic or aspects of it. This will involve study of four actual texts, and also model a form of preaching and teaching which is both expository of the text and severely practical and relevant to our needs. I have not included the full text of sermons or addresses, rather the outline with indications of application. (However, the full text of a sermon 'A Good Minister', expounding 1 Timothy 4.6-16, will be found as an appendix on pp. 110–17.)

Case studies

OVERSEERS AND DEACONS – WHO'D BE A LEADER? (1 Timothy 3.1-15)

Introduction: verse 1   ambition can be right (but remember Jesus' servant model)

                    verse 15   these instructions are given so that Christians will know how to conduct themselves in God's household, the church of the living God.

(1) Personal life

above reproach (v.2)	–	not open to justified criticism
temperate, self-controlled	–	under control, sensible, discreet
respectable, worthy of respect (vv.2,8)	–	dignified, serious
sincere		
no drunkard (vv.3,8)	–	see Chapter 9
no lover of money (v.3)	–	see Chapter 9; honest (v.8)

(2) Home life

husband of one wife (vv.2,12)	–	faithful in marriage
managing the family well (vv.4-5,12)	–	teaching children obedience and respect
not violent but gentle (v.3)	–	violence against spouse, children or others is increasingly being recognized as a real problem
not quarrelsome	–	rather a peacemaker
hospitable (v.2)	–	literally, a lover of strangers

(3) Church life

able to teach (v.2)	–	see also verse 9 keep hold of the deep truths of the faith with a clear conscience. Grasp it and give it!
not a recent convert (v.6)	–	to protect against pride. See also verse10 – they must first be tested.

(4) Community life

a good reputation with outsiders (v.7)	–	to avoid disgrace and the devil's trap.

PASTORS AND TEACHERS (Ephesians 4.1-16)

Introduction: Although all God's people are called to serve (minister) in the world and the Church, God gives in and to the Church some gifts of leadership of different kinds (v.11). This passage is addressed to the whole people of God – which includes its pastors and teachers. Spirituality is fundamental – Christian discipleship and ministry is based on an intimate relationship with God in Christ and by the Spirit.

(1) spiritual character (vv.1-2)

live a life worthy of the calling you have received – to be in the people of God, the body of Christ, the community of the Spirit.

humble, gentle, patient, bearing with one another in love – the fruit of the Spirit, the Christ-like character (Galatians 5.22-26).

(2) spiritual unity (vv.3-6)

Christian leaders often act like lone-rangers, individualists, with an arrogant conviction of a personal hot-line to God.

make every effort – unity is the mark of the Spirit, division is the devil's work.

theology has practical implications for behaviour – there is (only) one body, one Spirit, one hope, one Lord, one faith, one baptism, one God and Father of all.

(3) spiritual gifts (vv.7-11) *charismata*

given to each Christian – not just to some

the gifts are of grace – (God's undeserved love) so there can be no place for pride.

as Christ apportioned – just as the Holy Spirit is sent by Jesus through the Father's promise (Luke 24.49).

very varied (v.11) many others are listed in Romans 12 and 1 Corinthians 12 and all are valuable.

(4) spiritual vision (vv.12-16)

why does the risen Christ give apostles, prophets, evangelists, pastors and teachers?
 to prepare God's people to serve God
 so that the body of Christ is built up
 so that we move towards maturity – the fulness of Christ.
 What a vision! What a task!

SHEPHERDS OF GOD'S FLOCK (Acts 20.17-35)

Introduction: Paul's last words to the elders of the Ephesus church.

Note his emphases – after three years with them (v.31)

(1) the priority of preaching

verse 20   without hesitation (and v.27)

helpful to you

publicly, and in the privacy of their homes

about the divine initiative	–	God's grace (vv.24,32)
human response	–	turning to God in repentance and faith in our Lord Jesus (v.21)
the kingdom	–	(see p.38) the reign of God in the whole of life
the whole will of God		(see p.38) balanced teaching

(2) the place of suffering

due to persecution (vv.19,23)   tears

due to pastoral concerns (vv.30-31)   tears

beware of 'success stories', remember the tears of both Jesus and Paul

(3) the pattern of leadership

elders (v.17), overseers and pastors (shepherds) (v.28)

always on guard, keeping watch (vv.28,31)

for yourselves	–	lest you drift away from God
for the flock	–	God's Church, bought with his blood

Conclusion: I commit you to God and the word of his grace which can build you up now and give you an inheritance for eternity.

LEADERSHIP (1 Peter 5.1-4)

Introduction: to the elders/presbyters (v.1)

(1) witness (v.1) of the gospel which includes

      Christ's sufferings   –   for our sin

      the glory to be revealed   –   because of the resurrection hope

(2) shepherds (vv. 2-4)

      it is God's flock – not ours (v.2)

      it is in the shepherd's care – overseers

        God is shepherd of Israel (Ezekiel 34; Psalm 23)

        Jesus is the good shepherd (John 10) and chief (v.4) but he delegates

      not forced (v.2)   –   or grudging (the martyr complex)

      but willing   –   enthusiastic, joyful, delighted

      not greedy for money   –   or fame or status

      but eager to serve   –   the Lord

                                    the people

      not lording it (v.3)   –   authoritarian, arrogant

      but as examples   –   (see p.31)

Conclusion: the Chief Shepherd will come (v.4)

              he will judge our ministry

              he will reward faithfulness – an eternal crown of glory!

5

Historical Developments

Understandings of ministry spring out of, or are built upon, a view or doctrine of the Church. Ecclesiology is the context of a doctrine of ministry. This is why early in the book we studied major characteristics of the Church (Chapter 2) and the nature of the discipleship of all the members of the Church (Chapter 3) before consideration of leadership and particular ministries.

Unhappily, the doctrine of the Church has been a source of controversy through many centuries of Christian history. Issues of orthodoxy and heresy, and discipline and order became embroiled with church power struggles, issues of personality and also matters of Roman Imperial (or anti-Roman) policy in the 'secular' realms. The early centuries were not a time of peaceful Church unity and placid harmony. It is important to know something of early Church history with its debates and divisions. All this was long before the major split between East and West (now seen in the Orthodox and Oriental Churches of the East and the Roman Catholic Church of the West). Then in the sixteenth century came the rift in the Western Catholic Church commonly known as the Protestant Reformation.

From this Reformation emerged the Anglican, Presbyterian, Congregational, Baptist and Lutheran traditions. At that time or in later centuries, there also emerged the Christian Brethren, Society of Friends (Quakers), Methodists, Pentecostals and numerous other 'Independent' groupings.

Many of these different Christian denominations have different understandings of ecclesiology. In fact some have significantly developed their ecclesiological self-understanding in their own history.[1] Thus, it is not surprising that there are widely different understandings of ministry and, especially, of the nature and meaning of ordination. There are differences of opinion between churches/denominations and within them, about the relative authority of Scripture and later tradition(s). All acknowledge the unique authority of the Scriptures themselves, but there are at least two major problems. Firstly, most scholars now agree that the New Testament does not exhibit one, clear pattern of church order. Secondly, even those churches and leaders who emphasize the *supreme* authority of Scripture (supreme, that is, over tradition and reason) differ over their interpretation of Scripture at this point. This is evidenced by the debates between Anglicans, Presbyterians and Congregationalists down the centuries.

There is another significant issue that has become more apparent in recent years. Many younger Christians (and some who are not-so-young) are either disenchanted with the historic churches or simply uninterested in commitment to any institutional dimension of church life. This may be a result of an ecumenical commitment, or post-modern suspicion of all institutions. The result is that a significant number of Christians have moved into Independent, House, or Restorationist churches[2] and/or have little or no loyalty to a denomination at all. They move to churches which suit their needs – in terms of liturgy, children's provision, cultural patterns and general doctrinal teaching. The rights and wrongs of this development may be debated at length – its character of consumer-choice, the meeting of needs rather than responsibilities; but on the other hand, many people travel to their other communities of interest, and the multi-cultural dimensions of society seem to grow ever more complex.

However, one area where this development is severely problematical is that of church leadership and ordination. Nearly every church recognizes that certain of its members should be set aside and recognized in some special way for the ministry of word and sacrament, of example, pastoral care and leadership. This recognition is commonly called ordination. Thus, churches recognize that however modest the demands required for ordinary membership, substantial requirements are necessary about the selection, training and recognition of the publicly accredited leadership. As we shall see (in Chapter 8) those who will be tested for ordination in the Church of England need to demonstrate not only personal spiritual maturity but also some real track record of responsibility and team-playing within, and support from, their local church. The modern habit of moving from church to church whenever something does not quite suit one's preference or perceived needs can become highly damaging for the development of the next generation of leadership.

We have already noted something of the variety of terminology used in the New Testament of leadership, and some of the confusions that have later developed.

In this chapter we look briefly at some of the most significant developments:

Ordained ministry

There are a variety of hints and clues in the New Testament about the origins of ordination. Some of these are outlined in Chapter 8 about selection. One of the clearest references is in 1 Timothy 4.14 'Do not neglect your gift, which was given you through a prophetic message when the body of elders laid their hands on you' (cf. 2 Timothy 1.6). The widely agreed understanding of ordination is the Church's recognition and authorization of a person to a particular ministry through the invocation of the Holy Spirit and the laying on of hands. This is a major responsibility in order that the proclamation of the gospel and the oversight of the churches is handed on with proper care and faithfulness.

Ordination is commonly to the ministry of word and sacrament and involves example, pastoral care and leadership. In the previous chapter on leadership there was no mention of special sacramental responsibility. The reason is that the chapter was evaluating the New Testament evidence rather than the later historical developments. The New Testament writers say nothing explicitly about who should baptize or who should preside at the Eucharist. Nevertheless, very quickly and universally from the second century, it became the norm for the bishop and/or the presbyter to preside and usually to baptize. This role in the sacramental life of the Church was seen as inevitable and important.

The bishops/presbyters represented more than the local church. They represented the Church universal – both in history and geography. Thus, they also represented the unity of the Church. The two dominical sacraments (i.e. instituted by the Lord Jesus himself) speak of the baptismal entry into the Christian Church both universal and local, and the eucharistic nourishment and continuance in that Church. It was both inevitable and important that the chief pastor(s) and teacher(s) should exercise oversight of these sacraments. Very quickly, issues of order and discipline, unity, heresy, and even 'excommunication' arose and were critically matters about which the people looked to the ordained clergy for leadership. This sacramental ministry is, of course, intimately related to pastoral care and instruction in the faith.

The elements of public recognition and public responsibility have led to the development of language about the ordained minister(s) being representative. This language needs some careful unpacking because it can be used in very different ways. Before we attempt that, we shall review some other aspects:

The *task* of the ordained ministers includes the responsibility to enable the Church to be true to its Lord and to its total dependence on Jesus Christ and his Spirit. They serve to build up the Christian community in Christ, to enable and strengthen its witness. God gives pastors and teachers to do just this, and so they play a vital role (Ephesians 4.11-13).

The House of Bishops (of the Church of England) recently produced an important Theological Statement on Eucharistic Presidency.[3] It suggests that:

> *the ordained ministry is best conceived as a gift of God to his Church to promote, release and clarify all other ministries in such a way that they can exemplify and sustain the four 'marks' of the Church* — *its oneness, holiness, catholicity and apostolicity.* The ordained ministry is a sign of, and a means of drawing out the four marks of the Church, helping to bring about and realize in others the different ways in which the Church can participate in the priesthood of Christ and thus in the purposes of the Triune God.[4]

The ordained minister carries a responsibility to:

- foster *unity* and be a focus of it;

- promote *holiness* and be a godly example;

- act representatively as a sign of *catholicity* and universality;

- promote faithfulness to the *apostolic* faith.

The history of the Church shows the value of having a *focus of unity* in a leadership person or group who are publicly and continually responsible for the healthy life and development of the people of God. This focus should be helpful and strengthening. It can be unhelpful if it is distorted by isolation. We shall devote a chapter to the issue of collaboration later (Chapter 7). One of the most obvious developments in the idea of a visible focus was the increasingly clear expectation that the ordained minister(s) would preside at the Eucharist or service of Holy Communion. In most churches (including the Anglican) this is invariable, while in others it is the norm with exceptions permitted.

The Bishops' Statement affirms that:

> the Eucharist is a means of a genuine sharing in Christ, of an authentic union with him. Here Christ renews his engagement with those he has claimed through baptism. This is expressed at the Last Supper in the giving of the bread and the cup: both effect a bond with Christ. It underlies the eucharistic theology of both Paul and John in the New

Testament – for them, it is axiomatic that that Gospel involves a sharing in Christ himself, in his life, death and resurrection, and it is against that horizon that they set the Eucharist (1 Corinthians 10.14-22; 11.17-34; John 6.25-58). This sharing is neither magical nor automatic: it is to be discerned and recognized (an important stress in Paul) and is bound up with the faith which is the gift of God (especially important for John). The Eucharist does not simply help the participant to meditate on the saving significance of the cross; it mediates the gift of Christ's saving presence. This was also fundamental for many of the mainline reformers, including Cranmer.[5]

This is, of course, essentially a corporate matter, a communal event. As the Church shares in Christ's body, it both expresses and renews its *koinonia* (fellowship) as the Body of Christ. When the ministry of word and sacrament are used in proper harmony, 'at the Eucharist, the identity of the Church is expressed, actualized and made visible in its four marks – its oneness, holiness, catholicity and apostolicity'.[6]

The *authority* of the ordained minister is not in the person of the minister; it is entirely derived from, and rooted in Jesus Christ himself. This authority is a gift of the Holy Spirit in order to expound the Word of God and build up the Church of God. The minister acts 'in the name of Christ'. Article XXVI of the Thirty-nine Articles speaks of ministers of word and sacraments 'not [ministering] in their own name, but in Christ's and . . . by his commission and authority'.[7] This authority should always be exercised in love and humility, if the temptation to become autocratic is to be resisted.

In the Catholic and Anglican traditions the authority of the ordained ministers has always included the power of absolution, that is, to declare forgiveness of sins to one who is penitent. The John tradition has the words of the risen Christ to his disciples 'Receive the Holy Spirit. If you forgive the sins of anyone, their sins are forgiven; if you do not forgive them, they are not forgiven' (John 20.22f.). Then, in the letter to James, those who are sick are encouraged to call the elders who will pray and anoint with oil in the name of the Lord, leading to healing and forgiveness of sins (James 5.13-16).

The Book of Common Prayer has an Absolution or Remission of Sins to be pronounced by the priest following the General Confession at Morning and Evening Prayer. It includes the words 'Almighty God . . . who . . . hath given power and commandment to his Ministers, to declare and pronounce to his people, being penitent, the Absolution and Remission of their sins: He pardoneth and absolveth all them that truly repent and unfeignedly believe his holy Gospel.'

Now, in the context of these brief considerations of the ordained ministers' task, role as focus of unity, and authority, we return to the complex issue of the nature of the *representative* dimension. This concept can be used in several quite different ways.

Firstly, are ordained ministers representative of *the Church*? As those specially selected, trained and accredited they clearly are seen to represent the Church in leadership of worship, in preaching, in administration of the sacraments and pastoral care. They are recognized as official spokespersons. They frequently have privileges in visiting hospitals, schools and prisons.

Secondly, are ordained ministers representatives of *Jesus Christ*? This question is more complicated. In the ministry of the word, the ordained (and also lay preachers) are acting as stewards, heralds and ambassadors, and so surely represent Jesus Christ to the degree that they faithfully re-present and apply his message and gospel. As preachers and pastors they call people to submit to Christ, the Teacher and Chief Shepherd. However, those in the catholic traditions particularly have spoken of the ordained priest as representative of Jesus Christ at the Holy Communion. This is highly problematical to most Anglicans in Evangelical traditions and to other Protestant or Reformed Christians. Some of the issues behind these differences will be considered later in this chapter (in the section on ministerial priesthood).

There has been extensive discussion through the centuries on whether the ordained ministry is to another order of being (ontological) or to exercise particular charisms of preaching and pastoral leadership (functional). The Bishops' Statement says 'Those who are ordained do not stand apart from the Church community; rather, those who are to be ordained are called from within the community, and are then returned to serve within that community, though standing in a new relationship to it.'[8] This new relationship is permanent and traditionally signified by the term *character*. However, in the Church of England, each minister is also licensed to a particular parish, locality or appointment.

The ontological dimension must not be over-stressed, but it does have important elements. The 'validity' of sacraments depends on order rather than on personal ability. The spirituality of the minister is to be stressed for effectiveness and not just 'skills'. All ministry is ultimately a matter of divine gift rather than of human endeavour.

The threefold order – bishops, presbyters, deacons

As we have already noted, 'the New Testament does not describe a single pattern of ministry which might serve as a blueprint or continuing norm for all future ministry in the Church'.[9] However, during the second and third centuries, a threefold pattern of bishop, presbyter and deacon became almost universally established. This historic pattern has continued through the centuries in the ancient Orthodox, Oriental, and Roman Catholic Communions. It was kept by the Church of England at the Reformation. Other churches have adopted various patterns. The Presbyterian tradition is based on eldership – some teaching and some ruling (administrative and pastoral). Other traditions have ordained elders for the ministry of word and sacrament and lay deacons for administrative (and sometimes pastoral) functions.

The threefold order itself has not been without considerable developments and variations in the different traditions. Originally it seems to have developed in the local community. However, quite quickly, the bishop began to exercise oversight across a larger area and/or more than one community. The idea of a diocese emerged from the model of a central city with its surrounding towns, villages and countryside. We shall now consider briefly the functions of bishops, presbyters and deacons.

1. *Bishops* are senior presbyters who exercise an oversight of an area/diocese (cf. p.28). This oversight will involve a safeguarding of the apostolicity of the Church's teaching, an ensuring that the sacraments are duly administered, that leadership ministries are properly ordered and pastoral care maintained. These involve a particular concern for discipline and ordination. The bishop has responsibility to maintain unity within the diocese and with other dioceses in the Province and beyond, to give strategic leadership in mission and in ecumenical relations with other churches.[10]

There have been problems with episcopacy in history when bishops have failed to fulfil aspects of these responsibilities and/or have been autocratic in leadership. This has led to some churches being very suspicious of episcopacy, especially of its perceived tendency to worldly glory and power. However, churches which do not have episcopacy have discovered the need and value of leadership which extends beyond the local community. Thus, for example, Methodists have area chairmen, the United Reformed Church has moderators and the Baptists have developed the office of superintendent. These officers fulfil various episcopal functions.

2. *Presbyters* (also sometimes known as priests) are ministers of word and sacraments in a local community (cf. p. 28). They preach, teach, baptize, preside at the Eucharist, pronounce absolution, exercise pastoral care and seek to build up the local church(es) in discipleship, worship and mission. They have a particular responsibility to inspire and equip the local church members to fulfil their own ministries in the church and the world.

There have been problems with local presbyters (vicars, pastors, ministers, priests) when they have not met these responsibilities and/or have been autocratic in their leadership. This has been a particular danger where the solo-pastor/minister has been the tradition.

3. *Deacon* is a title that has been used in a variety of ways. Some preliminary attention was given to its meaning and use in Chapter 2 (pp. 10f) and Chapter 4 (p. 28f.).

Deacons are a constant reminder to the Church of the serving role of all Christians. In the ordination service deacons are called to serve the Church of God, and to work with bishops and priests in caring for the poor, the needy, the sick, and all who are in trouble. They are encouraged to strengthen the faithful and preach the word of God in the places to which they are licensed. Deacons assist the priests with whom they serve, in leading worship and in administering Holy Communion. They may baptize and do such pastoral work as is entrusted to them. Thus deacons have a teaching, liturgical and leadership role.[11]

Some churches (particularly Baptist and some Congregationalists) have as deacons lay people who assist the pastor(s), minister(s) or elder(s) with administrative and (often) certain pastoral responsibilities. However, the historic churches with roots earlier than the Reformation treat the diaconate as an ordained ministry. The way this is worked in practice has varied, is controversial and often unclear. Many churches (including the Church of England most of the time) use the diaconate essentially as a one-year apprenticeship or probation before ordination to the presbyterate. This is sometimes called a transitional diaconate. The term is slightly misleading because, of course, a presbyter does not cease being a deacon. Nevertheless, the point is essentially valid – the diaconate has been widely seen as the first step in the *cursus honorum*, the ladder of hierarchy. The Roman Catholic Church, some Provinces of the Anglican Communion and several other churches around the world have recently sought to renew this order with a distinctive or permanent diaconate. These ministers usually combine assistant liturgical (and sometimes teaching) roles with responsibilities for pastoral care or social welfare institutions and/or administration.

All this is quite problematic both within churches and in their ecumenical dialogues. In the Church of England, at the time of writing, there are only a very small number of 'distinctive deacons' while there are nearly 10,000 specially licensed lay preachers (Readers) and several thousand pastoral assistants. There are also the Church Army Evangelists. One of the as yet unresolved questions is how any renewed distinctive diaconate in the Church of England might relate to these other very significant accredited ministries which have systems of selection, training and episcopal (or diocesan) authorization and/or commissioning.

'The threefold pattern stands evidently in need of reform' said the influential report *Baptism, Eucharist and Ministry* (BEM).[12] However, it remains by far the most significant historical tradition of ministerial pattern, and continues as a fundamental element in ecumenical discussions. Famously, the Preface to the Ordinal in the *Book of Common Prayer* declared 'It is evident unto all men (sic) diligently reading Holy Scripture and ancient authors that from the apostles' time there have been these orders of ministers in Christ's Church: bishops, priests and deacons.' It certainly is clear that the threefold pattern is evident in the letters of Ignatius of Antioch in the first decade of the second century. But the evidence of the New Testament leads many scholars to find a twofold order of elders (= bishops) and deacons.

If this is so, how did the threefold pattern emerge so rapidly and comprehensively? One suggestion is that the individual bishop was a practical response to the need for a leader among the presbyters and a single focus of unity in teaching, the Eucharist and responsibility for church property. However, the evidence is not compelling. Another answer is widely supported by second-century writers. It is that the first bishops were appointed by the apostles themselves in order to provide for a continuity of leadership after their deaths. If episcopacy was an apostolic institution, it would answer the question at the beginning of this paragraph. It would mean the assertion in the Ordinal of the *Book of Common Prayer* is defensible, and would justify the ecumenical weight put on the continuance of the pattern.

Ministerial priesthood

We made some preliminary study of the concept of priesthood in Chapter 2. We noted that the word is *not* used in the New Testament specifically of the ordained ministers. It *is* used of Jesus Christ and of the Church as a whole. So it is quite uncontroversial for BEM to say:[13]

> Jesus Christ is the unique priest of the new covenant. Christ's life was given as a sacrifice for all. Derivatively, the Church as a whole can be described as a priesthood. All members are called to offer their being 'as a living sacrifice' and to intercede for the Church and the salvation of the world. Ordained ministers are related, as are all Christians, both to the priesthood of Christ, and to the priesthood of the Church.

However, what is debatable and controversial is whether the ordained presbyters have a particular ministerial priesthood, and, if so, how this should be described and practised. There are broadly two approaches: the more *'Catholic' position* is that the ordained presbyters speak not only in the name of the Christian community but in the name of Christ himself in relation to the community. Their ministry is not simply delegated by or derived from the community. It is argued that theirs is a distinctively different form of priestly ministry in that it 'is an appointed means through which Christ makes his priesthood present and effective to his people'.[14] The Report, *Priesthood of the Ordained Ministry* goes on to say:

> Their (episcopal and presbyteral) ministry may be called priestly in that it is their vocation to help the whole people to realise their priestly character. Through the ministry entrusted to them by the Lord, the Holy Spirit makes present to Christ's people the fruits of his priesthood and once-for-all sacrifice, namely the forgiveness of sins, access to the Father and grace to offer the sacrifice of themselves. This ministry is particularly focussed in the proclamation of the Gospel, in the ministry of baptism and reconciliation and in presiding at the offering of the eucharist. These are ordinances through which human beings are visibly incorporated into Christ's Body and sustained as members of the reconciled and reconciling community. It is in the particular relationship of the eucharist and the ministry of reconciliation to the sacrifice of Christ that the priestly character of the ordained ministry is most evident. This ministry is priestly because through it God makes present to his people the work of Jesus Christ, the mediator who brings humanity to God.

The Report ends[15] by suggesting that the Church of England's

> understanding of ministerial priesthood today is plainly expressed in the central prayer at the ordination of priests in the *Alternative Service Book* (1980).

> Almighty Father, give to these your servants grace and power to fulfil
> their ministry among those committed to their charge: to watch over
> them and care for them; to absolve and bless them in your name, and
> to proclaim the gospel of your salvation. Set them among your people
> to offer with them spiritual sacrifices acceptable in your sight and to
> minister the sacraments of the new covenant. As you have called them
> to your service, make them worthy of their calling. Give them wisdom
> and discipline to work faithfully with all their fellow-servants in Christ,
> that the world may come to know your glory and your love . . .

There is no doubt that aspects of this tradition and interpretation have been strong and influential in the Church of England particularly since the nineteenth-century Anglo-Catholic revival. It is a tradition and vision of Christian ministry which has inspired and nourished whole generations of Anglican clergy.[16]

The BEM Report seems to lean in this direction where it continues the section quoted above. Presbyters 'may appropriately be called priests because they fulfil a particular priestly service by strengthening and building up the royal and prophetic priesthood of the faithful through word and sacraments, through their prayers of intercession, and through their pastoral guidance of the community.' [17] There are several elements of this position that have been much debated and remain substantially unresolved.

The more 'Reformed' tradition in the Church of England argues that the concept of a ministerial sacrificing priesthood is unscriptural and un-Anglican.

We have seen earlier that the word 'priest' can either be a contraction of presbyter (elder) or the English translation of the Greek *hiereus* and Latin *sacerdos* which mean 'one who offers sacrifice'. The traditional and official teaching of the Roman Catholic Church uses the word 'priest' in this sacerdotal way, whereas, it is argued the Anglican Reformers used it as equivalent to presbyter.[18] However, it is now almost universally agreed that Jesus Christ perfectly fulfilled all that was needed to atone for human sin, his priesthood is complete, and his sacrifice on the cross can neither be added to nor repeated (see Hebrews 7.23-28; 9.24; 10.1-22).

It may well seem quite extraordinary that the word 'priest' was never used in the New Testament of official ministers. The early Christians knew the weight of many centuries of Jewish priesthood and the parallels in numerous other religions. However, the concept of priesthood was applied to the whole Christian community rather than to a priestly caste. The whole Church of God was called to pray for and witness to the world. Both of these activities are described in priestly terms in Romans 15.16 and Revelation 8.3ff.[19]

How then did the language of ministerial priesthood develop in the third century onwards? It almost certainly came through *analogy* with the Old Testament priesthood as the Eucharist was increasingly seen as a sacrifice offered on an altar. Thus, these two ambiguous developments fed each other – eucharistic sacrifice and ministerial priesthood. If this kind of language is to be used at all, it must be used with the greatest care. But even with the post Vatican II developments in the Roman Catholic Church and the various Agreed Statements of the Anglican-Roman Catholic International Commission, these remain very controversial matters.

Michael Green concludes his valuable discussion of this debate by saying:[20]

> In short, the Christian priesthood is, in F.D. Maurice's distinction (taken over by J.B. Lightfoot) *'representative* without being *vicarial'*. That is to say, when presbyters celebrate the Communion, they are exercising a double representative function which, as we saw, characterises the priesthood of all believers. They act on behalf of the Lord when proclaiming pardon and performing the actions with which Christ instituted the sacrament. They act on behalf of the people when they lead the prayers and praises and present the offerings of the congregation. They are acting *representatively*. They do not thereby take away the right of the people to direct access to God, nor of assuring the penitent of God's pardon. When the minister acts as God's mouthpiece 'he does not interpose between God and man in such a way that direct communication with God is superseded on the one hand, or that his own mediation becomes indispensable on the other.' And when the minister acts as the mouthpiece of the congregation, as 'the delegate of the priestly race . . . here too his function cannot be absolute and indispensable. It may be a general rule . . . that the highest acts of congregational worship shall be performed through the principal officers of the congregation. But an emergency may arise when . . . the layman will assume functions which are otherwise restricted to the ordained ministry.' Such is Bishop Lightfoot's conclusion.[21] I do not believe that any other is consonant with scripture.

Since the sixteenth-century Reformation, the Church of England has sought to be both Catholic and Reformed. At its best that does not mean a careless compromise, but rather a principled agenda to take what is right and best of those traditions and weave them together. That is not an easy task. Thus, with respect to the issue of ministerial priesthood the questions are 'How catholic?' and 'How reformed?' It might be helpful to some readers to see the discussion as involving a spectrum of views:

Baptist	Anglican	Anglican	Roman
Methodist	Reformed	Catholic	Catholic
United Reformed			

But the diagram would be misleading about many individuals in each of these churches or broad categories.

There are real issues of disagreement here. We do nobody any favours either by fudging the issues or by unnecessarily polarizing them. This latter problem is often the consequence of exaggerating the position of someone from a different tradition.

Varieties of ordained and other accredited ministries

In the Church of England ordained ministers are often known as clergy, clerics or clerks in holy orders. The most common and well-known form of ordained ministry is the local *parish* priest who is usually a vicar, rector (the distinction is now only historical) or priest-in-charge of a parish. A vicar or rector may be called the incumbent (officeholder of the benefice, i.e. the appointment or living). She or he may have an assistant curate.

Curates come in two main categories. When ordinands have finished their training at theological college/course, they are ordained and appointed as curate to a parish (normally) where they 'serve a title' for three or four years in a training position. Sometimes (but much more rarely nowadays) they serve a second or senior curacy in another parish.

As increasing number of clergy work in *Teams* or *Groups*. The 1983 Pastoral Measure defines them. *Team Ministry* comprises a rector and one or more team vicars, who share 'the cure of souls', and may have other lay or ordained ministers who share in the 'pastoral care'. There will be a single benefice comprising one or more parishes. The rector may have a freehold or a term of years, while all other members of the team will be licensed or given permission by the bishop. In the case of vicars, their licence will be for a term of years.

A *Group Ministry* comprises a number of incumbents or priests-in-charge of independent benefices. They will meet as a chapter, the chairman of which may either be elected or appointed by the bishop.

There are several hundred Team or Group Ministries across the country. They can encourage collaboration, development of varying specialist gifts and enable pastoral reorganization when there is a reduction in the numbers of stipendiary clergy. A criticism that has been levelled is that the legislation focused on the clergy, but where the lay people play a full part, these provisions are very valuable.

The Church of England has been imaginative and innovative in many other areas of ministry in recent decades. The accusation is sometimes made that changing the Church is like turning an oil tanker at sea because the process is so slow and tedious. In this area (and others) I believe the accusers often fail to investigate fully and so analyse all the evidence.

We shall be looking at the development of *women's* ministry in the next chapter. The progress may be regarded as tardy but it has been remarkable in terms of Readers (from 1969) deacons (from 1987) then priests (from 1994) with large numbers now incumbents of parishes or senior chaplains. Full details of these and all ministry numbers are provided annually in the booklet *Statistics of Licensed Ministers.*[22]

Some clergy are not in parochial ministry but in a *sector* ministry. Many of these are employed by a bishop or diocese (or nationally by the Archbishops' Council) as officers of particular departments and/or advisers in a particular area of mission or ministry. Examples are: vocations, directors of ordinands, ministry development, mission, children/youth work, education, evangelism, communication, social responsibility, community development, ecumenical relations, race and inter-faith issues, industrial and rural affairs (some of these posts may, of course, be filled by lay people). Many of these officers/advisers combine their specialist sector work with a parochial responsibility. These *'dual-role'* posts are increasing (probably over 1,000) in number as the total of stipendiary clergy continues to fall. One of the problems with a dual-role appointment (e.g. 50:50) is that one or both parts 'demands' more than its share (e.g. 50:75 or 60:60). A very clear job description is needed for *both* roles.[23]

Clergy are also employed as *chaplains* in or by various kinds of institutions. The main ones are hospitals (see the story in the Introduction), prisons, the armed forces, schools, universities and industry/commerce. They may be employed under contract by the relevant Government department or by a hospital Trust or an educational institution etc. They may be full-time or part-time, paid or honorary.[24]

For centuries there have been clergy who do not receive payment (stipend) from the Church, i.e. *non-stipendiary*. Paul, the apostle, resumed his trade of tent-making during at least one period of his missionary ministry so that he would not have to rely on the financial provision of others (see Acts 18.3; 20.34-35; 1 Corinthians 4.12). In the Church of England there was a strong tradition up to the middle of the twentieth century that was either totally opposed to or, at the very least, highly suspicious of non-stipendiary ministry. Partly this was because the ordained ministry was seen as a profession. However, in the 1950s the influence of pioneers like Roland Allen and of the worker-priest movement in France led to experimental developments especially in the diocese of Southwark, changes in the law and finally Bishops' Regulations (1970) for selection, training and deployment.[25]

There are different models for this form of ministry. The first (and most common) sees the focus primarily in the parish as auxiliary/supplementary to the incumbent. It is a fact that a considerable number of non-stipendiary clergy transfer into 'full-time' stipendiary parish or chaplaincy ministry. The second model sees the place of 'secular' work as the main focus, and the preferred designation is 'ministry in secular employment'. Some argue this has the advantage of more of a kingdom-focus rather than a church-focus. Others question whether this ministry is significantly different from what every Christian is called to in their daily discipleship (see Chapter 3). The third model is that of 'retirement ministry'. Many clergy retire, but are still able and delighted to offer substantial time and experienced skills to assist in parishes and deaneries.

There is widespread discontent with the title 'non-stipendiary ministry (NSM)' but no agreement as yet on an alternative. One or two dioceses use 'self-supporting ministry'. Sometimes doubts are still raised about the adequacy of 'part-time' non-residential training which is the way almost all NSMs are prepared for ordination, and about issues of commitment and accountability. However, there is no doubt that in many parishes and other situations the ministry of these clergy is deeply valued by stipendiary colleagues and lay people.

Another variant of non-stipendiary ministry adopted more recently is the *local* version. Originally known as local NSM (LNSM), it is now termed *ordained local ministry* (OLM).[26] The ordinands for this category are normally selected with a strong local emphasis, trained locally in the diocese with a strong emphasis on the local context, and are ordained for ministry in their local parish or community. The development is not universally approved, and each bishop and diocese makes the decision about whether to have an OLM scheme. One of the major and attractive elements of OLM is the way in which parishes are encouraged and enabled to develop a local ministry team of mainly lay people, out of which one or more may be selected for this form of ordained ministry. At the time of writing eighteen dioceses have approved OLM schemes. In both urban and rural areas it is becoming a significant development in mission and ministry strategy.

The ministry of *deacons* has already been considered. The Greek word *diakonia* was examined in Chapter 2 and the ministry of the deacon discussed earlier in this chapter as part of the historic threefold order. It was pointed out that there is a renewal of distinctive diaconate ministry in several countries and churches at the moment. The Church of England is again examining the issue at the time of writing. One of the questions is how such a renewed ordained diaconate would or should relate to the office of (lay) Readers and the ministry of pastoral assistants which are considered below.

All the varieties of ministry we have so far considered have been ordained – priest or deacon. We now move to accredited lay ministries. There is a kind of spectrum of ministries. It may be represented thus:

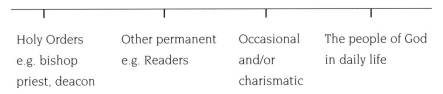

Holy Orders	Other permanent	Occasional	The people of God
e.g. bishop	e.g. Readers	and/or	in daily life
priest, deacon		charismatic	

Accredited lay workers are selected and trained in the same way as ordinands, and then, like clergy, may be employed by a diocese or be non-stipendiary. There are very few people in this category or receiving a vocation to it.

The *Church Army* is a mission society of the Church of England. It selects and trains women and men for the Office of Evangelist. They are commissioned by the Archbishop of Canterbury and most of them are employed in parish or diocesan posts. Some have traditionally worked in areas of social welfare, e.g. hostels for homeless people.

Readers (formerly known as lay readers) exercise a ministry of preaching, teaching and leading worship. Many will add to this aspects of pastoral care and a considerable responsibility for taking funeral services with its related ministry of care for the bereaved. There are nearly 10,000 active Readers now, and the numbers continue to rise. The title is often regarded as unsatisfactory but no alternative commends widespread assent. At least one diocese uses the designation 'Licensed Lay Minister'. The historical origin of the name Reader is, of course, from their reading of Morning or Evening Prayer and reading of sermons. It is now misleading because many other lay people read the lessons/scripture passages and lead intercessions. Readers are a major resource of trained and accredited ministry[27] Their ministry is most effective, not when they are used to fill in gaps in the absence of clergy but when they are honoured members of ministry teams.

Pastoral assistants are a fast-developing accredited ministry in some dioceses. These women and men are chosen for their pastoral concern and sensitivity and carefully trained to join the pastoral leadership team in a parish. They have widespread responsibilities in many aspects of pastoral care – in its individual, family and community dimensions.

Evangelists are also being trained and accredited in some dioceses. Unlike the Church Army evangelists, they will be voluntary and 'part-time'. The Church of England is increasingly adding to its essentially pastoral mode of ministry the mission and evangelistic modes. These lay people demonstrate a deep concern to share the Christian faith. They are further trained both to do this effectively, and to equip others to do it also[28] (see the section on mission in Chapter 3).

The *religious orders* may include both ordained and lay members. Monks and nuns are called to live in religious communities. There are several varieties of community working in England and other countries. Some are primarily committed to prayer, while others are involved in a whole range of ministries – evangelistic, educational and welfare. The members accept a disciplined pattern of life and some take vows of poverty, chastity and obedience.

The historical developments have been many and varied. Within the broad tradition of catholic order, the Church of England has, in recent years, sought increasingly to act imaginatively in seeking a ministry strategy for a missionary church.[29]

6

Women – In Leadership

Is it an issue?

Some readers may be offended that I have included a chapter on this subject. They will say that it is not (or ought not to be) an issue. They will say that even raising the question now about whether women can be leaders, ministers, pastors, preachers or priests is a sign of a dinosaur mentality. If pressed, they will point to the developments of women's rights in our society, to the developments of women's ministry in many churches, and to the theological truths that women were created in the same image of God, redeemed by the same sacrifice of Christ and are indwelt by the same Holy Spirit – as are men. It is not an issue, they will say. In fact, it is demeaning to women to have a chapter like this at all!

I hear these points, and in many contexts, they may be compelling. But there are other factors to be considered. The fact is, that for many people, for many Christians and for many churches there are unresolved issues with regard to women and leadership/ministry/priesthood. These continue to be areas of controversy, division and sheer misunderstanding. For example –

When people discuss issues in this general area, there are several *different agendas* (related, but different). Are we discussing a 'catholic' view of priesthood, a 'reformed' pattern of pastoral/presbyteral ministry, general issues of church leadership or the issue of public preaching? Again, are we talking about formal matters of leadership (which include ordination) or all areas of leadership in church life? Are we only thinking of church life or do the theological issues relate to family, community and 'secular' life generally? It is important that we are clear about what we are talking about, clear that we do not slide unconsciously from one issue to another, and clear also that when we espouse arguments for one position or another we think through with some rigour the consequences or implications of the position we are taking.

In the Church of England, there are many today who, for various reasons, *missed out on the debates* on the ordination of women in the 1980s and early 1990s. Some were too young, some not in the church, some not interested, some felt that the debates they did hear about were not relevant to their situation or to their theological framework.

A further reason for giving attention to this subject are the *new developments* in church life in recent years which alter the context of our thinking. Following the General Synod's decisive vote on the legislation on 11 November 1992 which opened the way for women to be ordained as priest/presbyter and therefore to be incumbents/vicars of parishes, the Church of England has experienced the ministry of 2,000 women priests – many hundreds as vicars or senior chaplains in hospitals or other institutions. This experiencing of women's ministry has had a profound effect on many.

However, in order to help those opposed to the development, the original legislation permitted parishes to pass resolutions not to have a woman priest or vicar, and provided financial provision for those who felt they must leave their ministerial appointment. In addition, and quite separately, the House of Bishops proposed an Act of Synod which included the provision of 'extended episcopal care' and the appointment of Provisional Episcopal Visitors (popularly known as 'flying bishops'). The work of the Forward in Faith movement has maintained the issue's high profile, and debate continues as to the propriety of the Act of Synod's provisions and /or how long they should continue.

Since women have been licensed as Readers, and ordained as deacons and priests, it is inevitable that attention is increasingly turning to the next issue of women in the episcopate. There are women bishops in other provinces of the Anglican Communion, and there are women in very senior positions in other churches.

Finally, there has been a very significant reaction amongst some conservative Evangelicals in recent years. Evangelicals in the Church of England (like Anglo-Catholics) were divided about the women priests' proposals. Many felt particularly marginalized because they thought the debate was largely conducted on catholic and/or liberal premises. Since 1992, conservative Evangelicals have increasingly distanced themselves from those sometimes called 'Open' Evangelicals who supported the ordination of women proposals. They have expressed their views through the organization 'Reform'. These developments have been strongly influenced through conservative elements in the Diocese of Sydney in Australia. Far from being seen as a (secondary) matter of Church Order, the issue has been magnified into both an assault on the authority of Scripture and the nature of the Triune God. On Scripture's authority, because, it is argued, the Bible is clearly against women exercising leadership/headship over men. On the Trinity, because, it is argued, the Persons of the Trinity are equal in dignity while Christ is subordinate to the Father, and this is the model for the male/female relationship. Some in these groups are also prohibiting women from preaching or teaching to congregations or audiences which include men.[1] The issues of women in authority have, thus, become associated (even entangled) with suspicion about the Church's confidence in, and exposition of, Scripture, its commitment to credal orthodoxy, and, particularly, its alleged liberalizing views on homosexual practice.

It is for all these reasons that I believe a chapter on this issue is needed. It is not only for those who are opposed to, or anxious about, women in leadership, but also for those who are in favour. It is vital that future relationships and debate are conducted in a proper spirit and with a proper methodology which takes the authority of scripture and appropriate principles of interpretation with the utmost seriousness.

The story so far

Through many centuries and across the world women have suffered oppression and injustice from men. It is a tragic and harrowing story – but it is a story little told and little known. Men have controlled the levers of power, men have made the laws, men have written the histories and controlled the publishing houses and the organs of the media. Christianity has made a difference in many countries and in many cultures – but its influence has often been ambivalent, its prophetic stance confused and its reforming programmes unclear. In this respect, the Christian attitude to slavery is often a parallel story. Slowly, gradually reform has come, but the struggle has been immense, the forces of conservatism massive.[2] But reforms have come.

The emancipation of women in society

In Britain, women had very limited rights and opportunities at the beginning of the nineteenth century. The eighteenth-century Enlightenment theory of an individual's natural rights was a powerful factor in the development of feminist thinking. Women's movements in the nineteenth century were often allied to movements for the abolition of slavery, for temperance (the abuse of alcohol has caused untold suffering to women and children) and to moral reform (the treatment of prostitutes and women prisoners is a particularly horrifying story when so many of them were essentially victims). Gradually, but very slowly in the nineteenth and twentieth centuries, various rights and opportunities have been won – political, legal, educational, economic and employment. But we must never forget the sheer tardiness of the reforms, the entrenched powers of conservative opposition and the sheer ignorance and bigotry of prejudice shown by so many.

The ministry of women in the Church

This has always been evident from the very beginnings of the Church, but often limited and confined. Cultural factors of patriarchy, inadequate biblical translation, and theologies which included fear of sexuality played their various parts in sustaining stereotypes which oppressed women and strictly limited the exercise of their gifts and abilities. For many decades, indeed centuries, women have fulfilled notable ministries of pastoral care and evangelism among other women, among children and to those on the margins of society – the destitute, the ill, the elderly. They have nursed, visited, taught children; they have been in religious orders and in foreign missionary societies – the list is endless. But there have always been strict limits and limitations.

A letter of Florence Nightingale written in 1852 expresses the frustrations of many women. She wrote:

> I would have given the Church my head, my hand, my heart. She would not have them. She did not know what to do with them. She told me to go back and do crochet in my mother's drawing-room; or if I were tired of that, to marry and look well at the head of my husband's table. 'You may go to Sunday School if you like it', she said. But she gave me no training even for that. She gave me neither work to do for her, nor education for it.

But changes have come. The developments of 'shared ministry' between clergy and lay people in public worship, home-groups, church councils and other areas of church life have opened up many opportunities. Many women have become church wardens and lay leaders in the synodical government of the Church. At present, the Chair of the House of Laity of the General Synod is Canon Dr Christina Baxter, Principal of the large St John's Theological College, Nottingham. Women were admitted as Readers (lay preachers and worship leaders) only in 1969 but there are now over 3,000 of them and their numbers continue to grow rapidly. The lay order of deaconess, was introduced in the 1860s and in the following 120 years hundreds of women were selected, trained and licensed to work in parishes. In the 1980s many hundreds were ordained deacon and then from 1994 ordained priest. They are vicars, priests-in-charge of parishes and senior chaplains in hospitals, prisons, universities and other educational institutions. They are cathedral canons, the Venerable Judith Rose is Archdeacon of Rochester, and, as I write, Canon Dr Joy Tetley has been appointed Archdeacon of Worcester. Women have been ordained in the (Presbyterian) Church of Scotland, the Methodist, United Reformed, and Baptist Churches. Also in Lutheran and Reformed churches in Europe. Anglican Provinces in America, Asia, Africa and Australasia have ordained women too.

I am unaware of any church taking this step which has regarded the development as anything other than a blessing and enrichment to church life.

The debates

The disagreements and debates fall into three categories:

> prejudice and ignorance;
>
> 'catholic' issues;
>
> biblical interpretation issues.

Prejudice and ignorance

There is no doubt that this has operated in the churches as well as in society. There has been enormous prejudice against extending to women political rights, educational opportunities and equal opportunities of employment in the professions. However, once the walls are breached, people wonder how such opinions were previously held. Women doctors, politicians and judges have had to win their way against great odds. Similarly, in the churches, once people have experienced the public ministry of women – in pastoral care, public worship, baptisms, weddings and funerals – their prejudice usually crumbles away. So it was with women doctors and lawyers.

Those who are in the theologically liberal traditions have usually been in the forefront of the campaigns for the emancipation of women, for women's rights in all areas of life, and for women to share in all aspects of the church's ministry. They have often been particularly sensitive to the 'signs of the times' and to God's unfolding purposes in our world today. They have been willing to question radically inherited tradition, custom and prejudice. These can be strengths and blessings. They can also be taken too far – so that inadequate attention is paid to Scripture and its proper interpretation, and to the catholic and historic dimensions of church life. Thus, a mere appeal to the 'spirit of the age' is quite inadequate. It would often lead Christians seriously astray.

'Catholic' issues

These concerns fall into three areas:[3]

(a)   The appeal to *tradition*. The traditional interpretation of Scripture has not included women in ordained ministry, and the tradition of most churches through most of history has followed that way. Tradition gives us roots in history and is not to be lightly cast aside. It reminds us that we are a part (a relatively small part) of God's people throughout the world and through many centuries. We need to be humble, and not arrogantly to think we know better than those who have gone before us. On the other hand, reformers (especially the sixteenth-century Protestant ones) have argued that tradition must not receive the same veneration as the Scriptures themselves. It is possible for traditional interpretations to be erroneous, and distorted by the patriarchal spirit of their age.

It is of course, true that the twelve apostles were all men. It is also true that most other leaders both in the Old Testament and in the Early Church were men. But there are some very significant exceptions – Miriam, the prophetess (Exodus 15.20); Deborah, the judge and prophet (Judges 4); Huldah, the prophetess (2 Kings 22.14-20); Mary Magdalene, entrusted with the message from the risen Lord to the disciples (John 20); Prisca (Priscilla) who, with Aquila, explained the way of God more accurately to Apollos, the powerful preacher (Acts 18.24-28 and Romans 16.3-4); Phoebe, deacon of the Church in Cenchrea, a great help to many including Paul himself (Romans 16.1-2); Junias, outstanding among the apostles (Romans16.7); Lydia, the business-woman who hosted the meeting of the believers in Philippi (Acts 16.13-15,40); and Philip's four daughters who had the gift of prophecy (Acts 21.9).

(b)   The *maleness of Jesus*. It is sometimes argued that the priest represents Jesus, particularly at the holy table (or altar) when 'offering the sacrifice' in the Eucharist (mass or holy communion).[4] Since Jesus was a man, only a man can represent him. This maleness of Jesus is no incidental matter. He represents the divine initiative in Christ. The incarnation reflects the creation pattern and order. This particular argument bristles with theological questions. The two most prominent issues are, firstly, does the priest (minister) at Holy Communion really represent Jesus? Was not Jesus the great High Priest who *fulfilled* the priestly atoning ministry of sacrifice for sin? If anything or anyone represents Jesus today, is it not the holy elements of bread and wine representing his body and blood, or is it not the whole people of God representing the royal priesthood (see p. 8f.), or is it not the preacher of God's Word who continues the preaching/teaching/pastoral ministry? Secondly, even if the priest does specially represent Jesus, is it maleness that is most significant, or rather *humanity* through the incarnation?

(c)   *Authority* and the *ecumenical* issue. Some who stand firmly in a catholic tradition do not believe that either of the two earlier arguments forbids women priests/pastors for all time. But they do argue that no one church (particularly a church claiming a ministry in the catholic tradition) has the authority to change the tradition unilaterally. A change of such magnitude would require an Ecumenical Council which included the Roman Catholic and the Eastern Orthodox and Oriental Churches. Such unilateral action gravely damages the catholic understanding and recognition of the Church's ministry and of relations between the churches. To this argument it may be replied: Catholic tradition must be open to spiritual renewal and reformation especially through the Scriptures. Thus the Church of England from the sixteenth century, and the worldwide Anglican family of churches arising from it, claim to be both catholic and reformed. The Roman Catholic Church denies the validity of the ordinations even of men in the Anglican[5] and other Protestant churches. In this situation of sad disagreement about the issues of authority and ministry themselves, it is quite unrealistic to wait for an Ecumenical Council. Each church may order its own ministry in the light of scriptural principle, catholic tradition and local circumstance.

The Church of England is catholic and reformed. A reformed church looks to the Scriptures as the supreme authority in matters of faith and order. So we now turn to issues of biblical interpretation.

Biblical interpretation issues

Many Christians have either assumed (after very little study) or concluded (after some study) that the Bible is entirely, or almost entirely, irredeemably patriarchal. It either teaches or colludes with the subjugation of women. When people take this view they then face a stark choice. On the one hand, some say that the Bible is culturally conditioned by its patriarchal times and that the practices and teaching in these areas can, and should, be ignored today. Or, other Christians will say all Scripture is obviously conditioned by its cultural contexts, but that was in the providence of God. We should not ignore what appear to be divine principles about the relationship and roles of men and women and the apostolic injunctions to the early Christians. It may be hard, counter-cultural and even perplexing, but it is part of obedient discipleship.

However, increasingly, Evangelical scholars have sought a third path which has questioned the way in which the premise is set up. Yes, they say, the biblical culture is patriarchal in many respects but not as much as superficial reading might indicate. We have already noted the striking examples in the Bible of women leaders (see p. 68). But beyond that, many of the passages often thought to indicate subjugation of women need to be looked at with much greater care. And before that, there are great and glorious theological signposts to which insufficient attention has been given.[6]

(a) *The New Testament passages.* The crucial New Testament passages fall into two groups – the family life group and the church life group. We haven't space to print the whole of these passages and, even more important, to put them in their context, but I have listed them and point out the context always before, and often after, which helps us to understand the significance of these passages.

> *The family-life group*
>
> | Ephesians 5.21-33 | in context of | 5.15 – 6.9 |
> | Colossians 3.5-19 | in context of | 3.1 – 4.1 |
> | 1 Peter 3.1-8 | in context of | 2.9 – 3.8 |
>
> *The church-life group*
>
> | 1 Corinthians 11.3-10 | in context of | 10.23 – 11.16 |
> | 1 Corinthians 14.34-35 | in context of | vv.26-40 |
> | 1 Timothy 2.11-15 | in context of | vv.8ff. |

I will quote the kernel verses to remind you of them.

A good example of the family-life group is Ephesians 5.21-25: 'Submit to one another out of reverence for Christ. Wives, submit to your husbands as to the Lord. For the husband is the head of the wife as Christ is the head of the church, his body, of which he is the Saviour. Now as the church submits to Christ, so also wives should submit to their husbands in everything. Husbands, love your wives, just as Christ loved the church and gave himself up for her.' Those passages in Ephesians, Colossians and 1 Peter speak of the submission of wives to their husbands and of the headship of husbands to their wives.

And then the church-life group – from 1 Corinthians 11 the kernel verses 3 to 5: 'Now I want you to realize that the head of every man is Christ, and the head of the woman is man, and the head of Christ is God. Every man who prays or prophesies with his head covered dishonours his head. And every woman who prays or prophesies with her head uncovered dishonours her head – it is just as though her head were shaved.' And in 14.33-35: 'God is not a God of disorder but of peace. As in all the congregations of the saints, women should remain silent in the churches. They are not allowed to speak, but must be in submission, as the Law says. If they want to enquire about something, they should ask their own husbands at home; for it is disgraceful for a woman to speak in the church.' And finally 1 Timothy 2 – the kernel verses 11 and 12: 'A woman should learn in quietness and full submission. I do not permit a woman to teach or to have authority over a man; she must be silent.' Those three passages speak about women having their heads covered; women being silent in church meetings; women being prohibited from teaching men and having authority.

What do these passages mean? What a passage says on the surface, and what it means, are not always exactly the same thing. There are many obvious examples. One of them would be Jesus saying 'If your right eye causes you to sin, gouge it out and throw it away' (Matthew 5.29). Christians do not encourage people to gouge out their eyes literally. What they say is that, although that is what it (literally) says, what Jesus was meaning, and what we should understand him as meaning, is that if your right eye causes you to stumble, you should go to enormous lengths to prevent that cause of stumbling through the eye. When we interpret Scripture, the higher our doctrine of its authority, the greater attention we must pay first to the question of metaphorical language and secondly to the issue of the situation in which it was written and the cultural factors that bear upon what is spoken about.

(b) *The first-century context.* So, let's look at this in its first-century historical context. It was an amazingly and radically new situation for women which Paul and Peter were addressing. *Josephus* was a Jewish historian of the first century. He said that woman is inferior to the man in every way. The *Jewish Talmud* classifies women with slaves and heathen and assumes them incapable of learning God's law – 'better for the law to be burned than to be interpreted by a woman'. A *Jewish man* each morning in his prayers thanked

God that he was not made a Gentile, a slave or a woman. *Plato*, the great Greek philosopher thought that a bad man's fate might be to be re-incarnated as a woman. This view of women that prevailed amongst so many of the Jewish rabbis and other leaders of society in the centuries just before Jesus Christ and immediately after was profoundly demeaning and dehumanizing. We now recognize slavery as an evil. Should we not be equally blunt in our judgement on such attitudes to women?

Contrast *Genesis* 1.27: 'God created human beings in his own image . . . male and female he created them'. God blessed them and God gave them *dominion* over the earth (vv. 26,28). Equally male and female in God's image. Equally male and female responsible for the care of the world, ruling together. The Hebrew word *ezer*, 'helper', used of Eve in Genesis 2.18 is a word sometimes used of an equal, more often of a superior, and is often used of God himself. It does not imply a junior or inferior assistant. This was distorted by the Fall. Male and female were alienated from each other and male domination arose, leading to oppression and subjugation.

Jesus came and reversed that situation with a revolutionary new attitude to women. He shared with them. They seemed to be in his travelling group, ministering to him and the disciples. He taught them – that was an incredibly new situation at that time. He taught the woman at the well, sinner and unclean as she was. He commended Mary who wanted to sit at his feet and learn from Him rather than Martha who was fulfilling the 'normal' domestic role. He accepted their ministry – the sinful woman who anointed his feet. He was gentle with them – even with the adulterous and with the ritually unclean woman suffering from the haemorrhage for so long. What a new attitude! (See John 4; Luke 10; Luke 7.36-50; John 8.1-11; Luke 8.43-48.)

When the *Day of Pentecost* came it was interpreted by Peter in terms of Joel: 'I will pour out my Spirit on all people. Your sons and *daughters* will prophesy'(Acts 2.17ff.; author's emphasis). Surely this means they will speak God's word, proclaim his good news. Like Huldah back in the Old Testament, like Deborah the judge. And then he repeats it – 'both men and *women* . . . they will prophesy'.

And then *Paul* came and in the great charter of liberty in Galatians 3.26ff. he says to men and women in the churches 'You are all children of God through faith in Christ Jesus, for all of you who were baptised into Christ have clothed yourselves with Christ. There is neither Jew nor Greek, slave nor free, male nor female, for you are all one in Christ Jesus . . . you are Abraham's seed, and heirs according to the promise.' And in Colossians 3.15ff. he says: 'as members of one body . . . Let the word of Christ dwell in you richly as you teach and admonish one another.'

Now these contexts, both historical and scriptural, need to be taken with great seriousness. In saying this, the aim is not to *evade* the passages quoted earlier but to *understand* them properly. It is those who do *not* take the wider scriptural contexts seriously who are being cavalier and careless with the Word of God.

What then of those passages that speak of submission of wives and headship of husbands and of women silent in church meetings? In the light of the creation intention of God (Genesis 1.26-28) and then of the extraordinary revolutionary actions and teaching of Jesus in the Gospels, Peter at Pentecost and Paul in his letters with regard to women, and not forgetting the women leaders in Old and New Testaments clearly within the plan and providence of God, a new line of interpretation has been developed. It suggests that several of these passages are better understood as instruction not to *abuse* the new freedoms women were enjoying, not to press their liberties to a position where they might appear not to share in Christian submissiveness to each other, or recognition of different roles in marriage, or of ignoring the possibility of public scandal and disorder. I repeat, this is not an attempt to *evade* the meaning but properly to *understand* it in its contexts – particularly the context of the whole of Scripture.

We shall look briefly at each of the five main issues:

(c) *The five issues*

1. *Submission*. It is *wives* who are told to submit to their *husbands* and not women who are told to submit to men generally, in every kind of situation. Note that the context in Ephesians chapter 5 is verse 21, where submission is mutual. Before anything about wives submitting to husbands, Paul says 'submit to *one another* out of reverence for Christ'. We are all to submit to one another – all Christians to all Christians. We are all to be submissive people, concerned about the cares and concerns of other people. This is the overarching principle. In fact, in the Greek text, the word 'submit' is in verse 21, but isn't in verse 22. That doesn't mean to say that the translators are wrong to put it in – it clarifies the meaning, but it does underline the fact that verse 21 is the overarching principle of which verse 22 is one application. We are all to submit to one another – we are to be submissive kind of people in the Christian fellowship – and within that, women must not forget they've got to submit to their husbands. In this new freedom they must not say 'O well, we are all one now and I needn't bother about my husband any longer and his

responsibility and his care.' Also note in this passage, and the equivalent passages that women are never instructed in the New Testament to *obey* their husbands. To submit, yes – but we have already seen that we are all to submit to one another. Children are instructed to obey their parents (6.1); slaves are instructed to obey their masters, (6.5) – but not women to obey their husbands. We are told that Sarah obeyed Abraham (1 Peter 3.6) but never is there a *command* that women obey their husbands. Therefore the meaning in the context seems to be that women, in their new found freedom, which is so glorious, and so radically new, should be careful how they live – not to abuse their freedom. We must all submit to each other, and supremely, a Christian husband and a wife must submit to each other.

This is worked out with respect to sexual intercourse in 1 Corinthians 7.3-5 where Paul says, essentially, 'Don't deprive each other, because your body doesn't belong to you. The man's body belongs to the wife and the wife's body belongs to her husband.' Therefore give in to each other, submit to each other. It's mutual. But within that mutuality, wives, in their new situation must not forget.

2. *Headship*. This is probably the most significant issue. Note first of all how very careful we must be about interpreting metaphor. It is a metaphor. Many people jump to the conclusion without giving it much thought that headship means authority or chief, as in head teacher. But leading scholars argue that it is more likely to be a metaphor indicating origin or source, as in the head of a river, from whence it flows. And so if you read Ephesians 5.22, the husband is the source, the origin of his wife, as Christ is the source, the origin of the Church, his body of which he is Saviour (cf. Colossians 1.18; 2.10,19). But it could also be a metaphor, a picture, of the unity and the close relationship between the two. Just as the head is closely joined to the body, so, the husband is closely linked to the wife, and Christ is closely linked to his Church. The metaphor could mean any of those things. But it is improper to insist that the metaphor must reflect all three of them. We must work out from the context which of these significances the metaphor has. In Hebraic thought, the directing control of the body was thought to be the heart rather than the head. Now since, as we have already seen, there is no command to women to obey their husbands, it may be more likely that the emphasis is on mutuality and that the metaphor means origin or source, or a close relationship. But secondly, even if the metaphor means authority, surely it refers to marriage rather than to all social relationships – all contexts. And even if it means authority, within marriage, or even if you wanted to push it

beyond marriage, what is authority and leadership in the Christian context? It is not domination. It is a loving, gentle, sacrificial, Christ-like, humble service. Jesus said to His disciples 'If you want to be great, if you want to be leaders, don't lord it over others, don't domineer over them – serve them.' So this would be the leadership/headship of a husband to a wife – loving service. If you're convinced that this headship applies in church life and in secular life, it is a loving service. But surely if it refers to authority at all, it refers to marriage, and within marriage, it's a loving service, rather than an authoritarian demand for obedience.

Thirdly, notice how careful we must be about comparisons, especially when they involve metaphor. There is a comparison with Jesus Christ. In Ephesians 5.24 it says: 'As the Church submits to Christ, so also wives should submit to their husbands in everything.' Does that mean that in the same way as the Church submits to Christ, in *exactly* the same way wives should submit to their husbands? Surely not. The authority of Jesus over his Church is due to his deity, his omniscience, his perfection. Husbands are not divine and they're certainly not omniscient or perfect. Surely it means that, just as the church submits to Christ because of his sacrificial love, so wives submit to their husbands who give sacrificial love to them. That is the point of the comparison. We have always to look for the point of the comparison, just as in the language of father and son. When we use father/son language we can be referring to literal reproduction. That is the first thing that comes to our mind, but when we read about the Father and the Son, with regard to God, that is *not* the point of comparison. The point of comparison is the closeness, the love and the identity of nature. We must be careful about the way in which we interpret metaphor, and the way in which we interpret anthropomorphic language, language of humanity that is used about God. And now on to the church-life group:

3. *Head covering*. The passage says that when a woman is praying or prophesying (and surely the implication is, when she is doing this in public) she should have her head covered. The context of the passage is Christian freedom. Paul has been talking about the question of freedom to eat meat that has been offered to idols and is now being sold in the market place. Paul's argument is that the Christian is free to eat – he or she doesn't have to ask all sorts of questions; but if it will cause stumbling to someone then this freedom should be curbed. Idols are nothing, so meat offered to idols doesn't really matter, *but* don't cause anyone to stumble. The context is Christian freedom and the restrictions to do with stumbling. So here, is not Paul saying, 'You are free,

you Christian women, in this new situation. But don't cause anyone to stumble by your freedom.' The historical, cultural situation required long hair and a veil to avoid scandal. In many situations in the world today, women would not be able to wear sleeveless dresses, or dresses that were above the knee in length. The principle is orderliness and propriety, not causing offence. The detail about the long hair and the veil is cultural.

4. *Silence* (see 1 Corinthians 14.33-35). The context indicates this cannot be a total prohibition of women speaking. In chapter 11, we see them praying and prophesying in public, and women have opportunity to contribute (v.26). All are encouraged to prophesy and tongues are not forbidden. The context again is order in worship. Tongues should be controlled, prophecy should be controlled, women's contributions should be controlled. Presumably this referred either to the shouting out of questions or to ecstatic chanting (that took place in some of the Corinthian worship of Bacchus). It may be better understood as 'keep quiet' rather than 'be silent'. Some of the women were abusing their new freedom.

5. *Teaching and authority*. The Greek word for authority in 1 Timothy 2.12 seems to indicate a domineering kind of authority. The context again is order in worship. Men are not to be angry or argumentative in free worship. Women are to dress carefully, to learn quietly and not insist on teaching in a domineering manner. They are not to abuse their freedoms.

I cannot deal with Pauline concessions in detail except to say that he was willing to make concessions (as at the Council of Jerusalem, Acts 15) to preserve fellowship. Literal interpretation sometimes proves too much as can be seen over the question of silence. Too often we have prejudices about masculinism, and psychological stereotyping between men and women. Too often we think of models of leadership as hierarchical and authoritarian when they can be shared and corporate, humble and servant-like.

The situation today

Women's emancipation in our society is social, political, economic, educational. If in the first century, Christian leaders were anxious to avoid scandal and unnecessary offence, we have to ask 'Where is the scandal now?' In the first century it was women abusing their freedom, throwing their weight around. Where is the scandal now? Isn't it that in our cultural situation, women are not given the freedom fully to use their gifts in the service of the Church?

There has been a remarkable development of women's public ministry particularly in the last 20 to 25 years (recounted earlier in this chapter, p. 64 and 66f.). It gives every appearance of being a strength and blessing to the mission and ministry of the Church.

There can be a developing clarity about the implications of the gospel. It was very difficult in the first century for Christians to come to terms with admitting Gentiles without them becoming Jews. Peter and Paul had arguments over it. It took a long while to get sorted out. Slavery took many centuries. The principles are there in the New Testament. But it wasn't clearly seen until the eighteenth century. Perhaps it is in our generation that we are seeing more clearly the gospel implications for the position about women.

Some have expressed anxiety about this development because they say other reforms are needed. But it may be replied that it is unnecessary and unfair to wait for all ministry issues to be put right. Some say 'sort out ordination; sort out priesthood; sort out single incumbency and shared ministry before women can be ordained.' Women have waited a long time, and the Church of England has devoted many years to investigating the range of issues.

These issues are still controversial for many. Women and men on both sides of the debates are offended and hurt. However, the Church of England now has several thousand women Readers, deacons and presbyters/priests, and the majority of Christian people are profoundly thankful to God for their ministries and the enrichment they have brought.

7

Working Together

Many a Christian leader still appears to be naturally a 'lone-ranger' or 'one-man band' or 'prima donna'. However, there has been a very significant shift in much Christian thinking and practice in the last thirty years or so.

'Working together' in different ways is a concept that in many parts of church life is seen as an issue of critical importance for many different reasons. It can be called shared ministry, mutual ministry, total ministry or collaborative ministry – and some will draw distinctions between some of these definitions or descriptions. There are different kinds of working together, for example:

- clergy of the same denomination – as in a Church of England Team or Group Ministry;

- clergy and lay people – as in a local ministry team (whether formally commissioned or informal);

- ecumenical – as in a Local Ecumenical Project or a local Churches Together group.

It is the working together of clergy and laity that was particularly addressed by John Stott in his lectures published as *One People – Clergy and Laity in God's Church*. He quotes the papal encyclical of Pius X (1906, *Vehementer Nos*): 'As for the masses, they have no other right than that of letting themselves be led, and of following their pastors as a docile flock.' He also quotes the Anglican Sir Kenneth Grubb: 'The Church of England does not give a strong impression of being interested in its laity: it seems either to ride them or to fear them . . . . It seems a fair assumption . . . that the clergy of the Church of England do not trust the laity, and, if this be indeed so, then there is no strong reason why the laity should not return the compliment.' [1]

It is little wonder that the Lambeth Conference of Bishops of 1958 said 'There is a growing recognition today that too sharp a distinction has been made between clergy and laity'.[2] Why has there been such a shift of thinking in many parts of the church? Many different reasons can be suggested:

1. There is so much *work* to be done, so the Church needs to mobilize lay people. A few may be paid as an administrator, musician, youth worker, verger, etc. but the large majority will be volunteers. Of course, there is a long history of lay volunteers as Sunday School teachers, visitors, choir members, cleaners, treasurers, etc.

2. It is sometimes suggested that shortage of *money* is a factor. The Church cannot afford so many clergy, and so we need to encourage lay volunteers to do what clergy used to do. Related to this is the decline in the number of stipendiary clergy in many churches.

3. It has been suggested that many lay people are looking *for opportunities of service* and/or leadership in their local churches. If they do not find opportunities there, they will look to other organizations where their gifts and energies will be welcomed.

4. The dangers of *clergy loneliness* are being increasingly recognized. This matter will be addressed further in Chapter 9. Loneliness can lead to the development of unhelpful characteristics, to overwork, to stress and to the attempt to do things without the appropriate wisdom, knowledge, or skill. In the light of this, it is good to share with others in many ways. In the Church of England, some clergy have, for many years past, encouraged their church wardens, their Parochial Church Council (or its Standing Committee) or some kind of staff team to be a shared leadership team.

5. *Lay development* has increased in a very marked way in recent decades. Lay people in their thousands are studying the Bible, Christian theology, counselling and many related subjects. They are experiencing Christian leadership in numerous ways – leading home groups (for Bible study, prayer, healing, ecumenical fellowship, Alpha, Emmaus, etc.), practical projects of social/community concern, church planting, baptism, confirmation, and marriage preparation, bereavement visiting, etc.

Several of these reasons (perhaps all) have significance, but we must also evaluate carefully biblical, theological and spiritual factors. There has been considerable attention to what the Bible has to say about working together.

Biblical case studies

We simply look at two stories:

Moses (Exodus 18.13-23)

> The next day Moses took his seat to serve as judge for the people, and they stood round him from morning till evening. [14]When his father-in-law saw all that Moses was doing for the people, he said, 'What is this you are doing for the people? Why do you alone sit as judge while all these people stand around you from morning till evening?' [15]Moses answered him, 'Because the people come to me to seek God's will. [16]Whenever they have a dispute, it is brought to me, and I decide between the parties and inform them of God's decrees and laws.' [17]Moses' father-in-law replied, 'What you are doing is not good. [18]You and these people who come to you will only wear yourselves out. The work is too heavy for you; you cannot handle it alone. [19]Listen now to me and I will give you some advice, and may God be with you. You must be the people's representative before God, and bring their disputes to him. [20]Teach them the decrees and laws, and show them the way to live and the duties they are to perform. [21]But select capable men from all the people – men who fear God, trustworthy men who hate dishonest gain – and appoint them as officials over thousands, hundreds, fifties and tens. [22]Have them serve as judges for the people at all times, but have them bring every difficult case to you; the simple cases they can decide themselves. That will make your load lighter, because they will share it with you. [23]If you do this and God so commands, you will be able to stand the strain, and all these people will go home satisfied.

(a) The *problem*. Moses had a problem and the people had a problem. We do not know whether they realized this before Jethro, Moses' father-in-law, saw what was happening and delivered his analysis and advice. Sometimes a visitor, a friend, an external consultant has a clearer view of what is happening. Jethro saw three issues that were problematical:

- *Overwork*. Moses was working hours that were too long – 'from morning till evening' (v.14). In English idiom, we might say he was working 'all hours'. He was attempting too much, trying to hear too many cases and adjudicate on too many issues. 'The work is too heavy' (v.18).

- *Loneliness*. Note Jethro's question 'Why do you sit alone?' (v.14), and his later analysis 'You cannot handle it alone' (v.18).

- *Inability to cope.* We would call it stress. Jethro concludes 'You will only wear yourself out' (v.18). Now that is a serious matter for any leader, but there are also serious consequences for others and Jethro adds that he will also 'wear out the people who are here'. This element can too easily be overlooked or minimized. The inability of any leader to cope has serious effects on colleagues and those looking to the leader.

(b)   The *solution*. It was providential that Jethro visited, observed what was happening, had the insight to realize the nature of the problem and the courage to tackle his son-in-law about it. 'Wounds from a friend can be trusted' says the wise man (Proverbs 27.6). It often takes real courage to speak up in a situation like this, and then, of course, real humility and grace to listen and to take advice. Jethro is quite blunt – 'What you are doing is not good' (v.17), 'Listen now to me and I will give you some advice, and may God be with you' (v.19).

Jethro's advice is that Moses should work together with others and share the load. It may sound obvious – but clearly it had not been sufficiently obvious to Moses up to this point, and it is clearly not sufficiently obvious to many Christian leaders today. Jethro advises him to 'select capable men from all the people – men who fear God, trustworthy men who hate dishonest gain – and appoint them' (vv. 21 ff.). He had to learn to delegate – shared ministry, collaborative leadership.[3]

(c)   The *consequences* spelled out by Jethro are threefold: 'that will make your load lighter' (v.22), 'you will be able to stand the strain' (v.23) and 'all these people will go home satisfied' (v.23). In modern jargon we might translate it as 'your stress levels will be reduced, you will avoid the likelihood of a nervous breakdown, and the whole enterprise will be successful'. But this is not mere management technique, it includes God's presence and God's direction (see vv.19,23).

There is a regular temptation for Christian people, including those in leadership, to over-spiritualize problems and ignore (sanctified) common sense. This problem is not met by more prayer, greater holiness or deeper consecration – it is met by correct analysis, humility and careful delegation.

The apostles (Acts 6.1-6)

In those days when when the number of disciples was increasing, the Grecian Jews among them complained against the Hebraic Jews because their widows were being overlooked in the daily distribution of food. [2]So the Twelve gathered all the disciples together and said, 'It would not be right for us to neglect the ministry of the word of God in order to wait on tables. ³Brothers and sisters, choose seven men from among you who are known to be full of the Spirit and wisdom. We will turn this responsibility over to them ⁴ and will give our attention to prayer and the ministry of the word.' ⁵This proposal pleased the whole group. They chose Stephen, a man full of faith and of the Holy Spirit; also Philip, Procorus, Nicanor, Timon, Parmenas, and Nicolas from Antioch, a convert to Judaism. ⁶They presented them to the apostles, who prayed and laid their hands on them.

(a) The *problem*. The apostles had a problem and the young church in Jerusalem had a problem. The problem only became obvious when a grievance arose and a complaint was lodged. This was a high-profile matter because it involved elements of both racial discrimination and an unfair use of the common fund for social welfare. The Greek-speaking Jews said that their widows were not getting fair treatment (vv.1-2). This was a weighty accusation because, if true, it undermined two major commitments in the Christian community – firstly, that racial discrimination is utterly unjustified because all the disciples are 'one in Christ' and receive the one Spirit; secondly, that the disciples were known as those who loved each other and cared for each other with a practical concern.

Now that was the presenting problem – and serious, by any standard. But there was another issue lying behind it. The clues are there. The disciples were growing in number (v.1). Surely, it was because of this (at least partly) that the apostles overlooked the growing problem of discrimination and unfairness. They were, to put it bluntly, over-working. They simply could not cope with the growing demands.

(b) The *solution* was recognized by the twelve apostles. The answer was to delegate the tasks, to share responsibility and leadership. Note that they thought through what their own priorities had to be (v.2) 'it would not be fitting for us to neglect the word of God in order to wait on tables'. So other people must be selected and appointed. It sounds so obvious, but in fact, the answer and the action only came after there was upset, grievance and complaint.

(c) The *consequences* were very considerable. Firstly, the apostles were able to devote themselves to their priorities of prayer and the ministry of preaching and teaching (v.4). Secondly, the church growth continued (v.7) 'so the word of God spread. The number of disciples in Jerusalem increased rapidly, and a large number of priests became obedient to the faith.' Thirdly, the new appointments encouraged a flowering of talent – Stephen became an impressive leader, apologist and martyr (6.8 – 8.3) and Philip became a most influential evangelist to Samaria and to the Ethiopian Chancellor of the Exchequer (8.4-40). Fourthly, harmony was restored to the church between the racial groups, and a real issue of injustice and pastoral care was urgently addressed.

Before we leave this episode, note the kind of people that were required for this task of financial administration and pastoral welfare – people of 'good repute', 'full of the Holy Spirit and of wisdom' (v.3). Integrity, spirituality and wisdom were in the 'person specification'. When they had been chosen with the approval of the whole congregation (v. 5), they were solemnly commissioned with prayer and apostolic hands laid on them (v.6). How often are these criteria and procedures followed today in the appointment of those to look after church finances, property and social and community projects, etc? Lower standards than these have led to terrible scandal among ordained and lay leaders, among both clergy, evangelists and treasurers! (See further in Chapter 9.)

Both Moses and the Twelve Apostles had to learn sharp and practical lessons about 'working together' with others. But these case studies have theological foundations.

Theological foundations

What has been seen in the case studies is not simply secular managerialism or worldly pragmatism. It is theologically and spiritually right at every point. Paul's letter to the Romans Chapter 12 has been used earlier (p.20) when we were considering the life of discipleship. But here we need to turn to it again. We are reminded that all Christians are called:

- to serve – sacrificially, with minds renewed and discerning the will of God (vv.1-2);
- to modesty and realism (v.3) about themselves and the limits of their abilities;
- to recognize the gifts, skills and functions of others (vv.4-6).

The theology is simple and clear. Working it out in practice is not always simple or clear. Most of us have considerable problems in practice over 'working together'. Clergy and other Christian leaders often find it particularly difficult. All too easily, they come up with practical objections.

Practical objections

These usually come in one of two forms:

1. 'It may be right in some places, but you don't understand my church or parish. We don't have those sort of people – with gifts and leadership'. I believe three questions need to be addressed:

- Has there been a tradition of church teaching – as in the case studies and theological foundations in this chapter?

- Has there been a prayerful and encouraging search for, and recognition of, people with a variety of gifts, skills and roles?

- Has there been a set of inappropriate stereotypes of leadership?

My experience in parish, deanery and archdeaconry indicates that wonderful gifts and abilities are there in the most unlikely people and circumstances including areas of great deprivation – but teaching, perception, imagination, risk-taking and encouragement are all required. But remember these features in Jesus' selection of the unreliable Peter, the tempestuous James and John and the traitorous Judas.

2. 'I just haven't got time for all that selection, training and encouraging business. You don't understand. There's so much to do, so much pressure and so many expectations. It's quicker to do the jobs myself!' This objector needs good friends, a spiritual director or soul friend, a bishop or adviser; who will very gently and patiently explore the layers of hurt through misunderstanding, through bondage to inappropriate expectations, through being let down. The dangers of this approach need investigating – spiritual, psychological, physical – dangers to the family and to the church. Very gently, certain practical and realistic steps need to be thought through and put in place to escape this prison. Help is needed! Don't wait for the breakdown! (We look at other aspects of this issue in Chapter 9.)

Working together is a real issue for many clergy and church leaders. The consequences are of major significance for the health, vitality and growth of the churches in Britain today.

8

Choosing Leaders

The choice and development of leaders is a major issue in many areas of life today – in politics, education, industry and commerce, etc. It is also a major issue in the Bible and in the Christian tradition. Good leaders are a source of strength and blessing, poor leaders provoke perplexity, weakness and uncertainty.

Before we begin to enquire into detail about selection procedures, there are some preliminary matters that may be clarified.

Presuppositions

Although, in some areas of selection, common sense is important and also much can be learned from wisdom and experience gained in other areas of life, there are some theological foundations that must be kept in mind:

1.   *God gifts* people for leadership, and gifts such people to his Church. The gift and skill of leadership is mentioned explicitly in Romans 12.8. Ephesians 4.11ff. says of Jesus Christ 'It was he who gave some to be apostles, some to be prophets, some to be evangelists, and some to be pastors and teachers, to prepare God's people for works of service, so that the body of Christ may be built up until we all reach unity in the faith and in the knowledge of the Son of God and become mature, attaining to the whole measure of the fulness of Christ.' Such gifts must be recognized by the Church and encouraged.

2.   *God calls* – It is reported that Paul says of himself 'I was appointed a herald and an apostle . . . and a teacher' (1 Timothy 2.7). Timothy is told 'Do not neglect your gift, which was given you through a prophetic message' (1 Timothy 4.14).

3.   *God empowers* – Jesus was empowered for his ministry by the Holy Spirit – 'The Spirit of the Lord is on me, because he has anointed me to preach good news to the poor ' (Luke 4.18). The disciples are told to expect 'power from on high' and 'power when the Holy Spirit comes on you' (Luke 24.49; Acts 1.8). Such power must never be taken for granted – for it can be withdrawn by God and can be quenched by us.

Patterns or the criteria for selection

Jesus' criteria for his disciples who became the apostles are not clearly spelled out. In fact the selection is quite problematic. They really were a very mixed bag. They were slow to understand Jesus' teaching, they showed lack of faith, they argued over their pecking order and, in the end, they deserted their leader. In character, understanding and determination they were frail. However, after Jesus' resurrection and the gift of the Holy Spirit we can clearly see the expectation that they would be missionary/apostolic preachers and teachers – 'make disciples, baptize, teach' (Matthew 28.19). They would be looked to for pastoral leadership – 'tend/feed my lambs' (John 21.15).

When the Early Church in Jerusalem was looking for leaders to handle the sensitive issues about social welfare distribution to the widows, the criteria were made very clear – 'seven men . . . known to be full of the Spirit and wisdom' (Acts 6.3).

The Ephesian elders were expected by Paul to guard themselves 'and the flock of which the Holy Spirit has made you overseers' and to be shepherds (Acts 20.28).

We have seen in Chapter 4 that the Pastoral Epistles speak of patterns of ministerial leadership which include the highest standards of character, the ability to teach, spiritual maturity, and the determination to be a disciplined servant of Christ and a humble example to others (1 Timothy 3 – 4).

The expectations of the Church of England are set out in three main ways. The *Ordinals* (services for ordination) speak in detail of teaching the Word of God, being examples of holiness and pastoral service to others (see Chapter 4). The *Canons* (of church law) include:

C 4 *Of the quality of such as are to be ordained deacons or priests*

1.   Every bishop shall take care that he admit no person into holy orders but such as he knows either by himself, or by sufficient testimony, to have been baptized and confirmed, to be sufficiently instructed in holy Scripture and in the doctrine, discipline, and worship of the Church of England, and to be of virtuous conversation and good repute and such as to be a wholesome example and pattern to the flock of Christ.

and

C 15 *Of the Declaration of Assent*

I(1) The Declaration of Assent to be made under this Canon shall be in the form set out below:

PREFACE

The Church of England is part of the One, Holy, Catholic and Apostolic Church worshipping the one true God, Father, Son and Holy Spirit. It professes the faith uniquely revealed in the Holy Scriptures and set forth in the catholic creeds, which faith the Church is called upon to proclaim afresh in each generation. Led by the Holy Spirit, it has borne witness to Christian truth in its historic formularies, the Thirty-nine Articles of Religion, the Book of Common Prayer and the Ordering of Bishops, Priests and Deacons. In the declaration you are about to make will you affirm your loyalty to this inheritance of faith as your inspiration and guidance under God in bringing the grace and truth of Christ to this generation and making Him known to those in your care?

DECLARATION OF ASSENT

I, A B, do so affirm, and accordingly declare my belief in the faith which is revealed in the Holy Scriptures and set forth in the catholic creeds and to which the historic formularies of the Church of England bear witness; and in public prayer and administration of the sacraments, I will use only the forms of service which are authorised or allowed by Canon.

Thirdly, the bishops have agreed the following Summary of the *Criteria* for Selection for Ministry in the Church of England:

A   MINISTRY WITHIN THE CHURCH OF ENGLAND

Candidates should be familiar with the tradition and practice of the Church of England and be ready to work within them.

B   VOCATION

Candidates should be able to speak of their sense of vocation to ministry and mission, referring both to their own conviction and to the extent to which others have confirmed it. Their sense of vocation should be obedient, realistic and informed.

C   FAITH

Candidates should show an understanding of the Christian faith and a desire to deepen their understanding. They should demonstrate personal commitment to Christ and a capacity to communicate the Gospel.

D   SPIRITUALITY

Candidates should show evidence of a commitment to a spiritual discipline, involving individual and corporate prayer and worship. Their spiritual practice should be such as to sustain and energise them in their daily lives.

E   PERSONALITY AND CHARACTER

Candidates should be sufficiently mature and stable to show that they are able to sustain the demanding role of a minister and to face change and pressure in a flexible and balanced way. They should be seen to be people of integrity.

F   RELATIONSHIPS

Candidates should demonstrate self-awareness and self-acceptance as a basis for developing open and healthy professional, personal and pastoral relationships as ministers. They should respect the will of the Church on matters of sexual morality.

G   LEADERSHIP AND COLLABORATION

Candidates should show ability to offer leadership in the Church community and to some extent in the wider community. This ability includes the capacity to offer an example of faith and discipleship, to collaborate effectively with others, as well as to guide and shape the life of the Church community in its mission to the world.

H   QUALITY OF MIND

Candidates should have the necessary intellectual capacity and quality of mind to undertake satisfactorily a course of theological study and ministerial preparation and to cope with the intellectual demands of ministry.

These criteria recognize that vocation depends not simply on personal faith but on the call of the Church and the grace of God.

Procedures for selection

We do not know how Jesus selected the twelve disciples and other close associates in his ministry in Galilee and Judaea. We do have accounts of him calling some of them from their trade as fishermen and Matthew from his tax-collecting.

However, following the resurrection of Jesus, we do find some interesting examples of selection procedures. After the loss of Judas Iscariot, the early believers decided to appoint a replacement. Five points of the procedure seem discernible from Acts 1.20-26:

- They found general guidance in the Scriptures (v.20).

- They agreed the criteria (v.21ff.).

- They proposed a shortlist (v.23).

- They prayed (v.24f.).

- They drew lots (v.26).

The appointment of the Seven (commonly called deacons) has already been considered in the previous chapter (p. 81f.). The following procedures appear in Acts 6.1-7:

- There was a problem which indicated a need (v.1).

- The twelve made a proposal which was approved by the whole group (v.2ff.).

- The brothers chose men according to clear criteria (v.3ff.).

- The candidates were presented to the apostles who prayed and laid their hands on them (v.6).

Another occasion of special commissioning takes place in the church at Antioch (in Syria) – see Acts 13.1-4:

- The general context was a church with prophets and teachers (v.1).

- The particular context was a time of worship and fasting (v.2).

- The Holy Spirit spoke – perhaps as a prophetic word to an individual or to several people but accepted by all. The message was explicit about the two men Barnabas and Saul who were to be set apart 'for the work to which I have called them' (v.2).

- The church fasted, prayed, placed hands on them and sent them off (v.3).

- The two were sent on their way by the Holy Spirit (v.4).

In these last two examples we find that prayer and the laying on of hands seem to indicate an ordination or formal commissioning. This second element is again explicit in 1 Timothy 4.14 which speaks of

> a gift not to be neglected
>
> given through a prophetic message
>
> when the elders laid on their hands.

The Church of England procedures are more varied and complex than many people realize. Before we describe these it will be helpful to think briefly about the main types of ecclesiastical polity, i.e. ways in which churches organize themselves and make decisions.

1. The congregation or parish. Baptists classically adopt a *congregationalist* polity.

2. The diocese led by a bishop. The Roman Catholics classically adopt this *episcopal* polity.

3. The nation with its assembly or synod. The Methodist Church in England takes most of its major decisions at its annual national Conference – *synodical* polity.

Although the Church of England is an episcopal church, it actually combines elements of all three types of polity – especially when it comes to the selection of leaders. Many leaders are chosen at the congregational or parish level, e.g. church wardens, the church council (PCC), local ministry teams, Sunday School teachers, etc. (Lay) Readers are nominated by vicar and PCC but with diocesan approval, training and authorization. Incumbents/vicars are appointed through a combination of the parish (through its representations and its representatives), the patron, and the diocesan (or area) bishop. Diocesan bishops are appointed at the national level (Crown advised by the Prime Minister after nominations by the Church's Crown Appointments Commission) but with strong input by the diocese in its representations and its four representatives on the Commission.

With respect to *ordinands*[1] there are five main stages in the selection procedures:

1. the *parish* support through vicar and senior lay people;

2. the *diocese* through the bishop and his DDO (diocesan director of ordinands) who might be assisted by vocation officers and examining chaplains;

3. the *national* Selection Conference when candidates are interviewed and assessed by three bishops' selectors. They make use of detailed references from parish, diocese and other sources and have guidance from a staff member of the Ministry Division. The Selectors make a recommendation (according to the criteria listed earlier on page 87–88) back to

4. the *diocesan* (or sponsoring) bishop who makes the final decision. This decision is to sponsor the candidate for *training*. So the next step is

5. the college or course *principal* writes a report to the bishop concerning the candidate and the success (or otherwise) of the training process.

Each of these stages is in the context of prayer and consultation. Where a candidate is successful, this leads to the Ordination Service with prayer and the laying on of hands, and the commissioning to a particular area of ministry.

No Selection system operated by human beings will be perfect but various safeguards and provisions are in place to minimize the effects of frailty and error. Note:

- the different stages with their complementary contributions;

- the collaborative nature of the system at every stage;

- conditions may be attached to a recommendation, which adds flexibility;

- a bishop may set aside (or over-rule) a recommendation and/or any condition(s);

- a candidate may return to a second (or even third) Selection Conference which will have a different staff.

In spite of all the prayer and the care, mistakes can be made.[2] Some people who are recommended and trained and ordained (or licensed) to a leadership ministry find severe problems and difficulties which can damage their ministry. These issues will be faced in the next chapter.

All Christians are called by God to ministry. Selectors look for *distinctive* signs that there is a call to *ordained* or *accredited lay* ministry within the Church.

Candidates must be seen to hear God's call to serve him in a particular ministry. They must be willing to surrender to that demand. The sense of call may have come in two different ways. Some will have seen the need for more people to serve in the ordained or accredited lay ministry. They will feel they have the necessary qualities and ought to offer themselves. This may be especially true in areas where the professional ministries seem particularly hard pressed. Selectors then want to be confident that such candidates have moved on from this realization and now feel personally drawn by God to meet the need.

Other candidates have a strong inward sense that they personally have been called by God to offer for a specific ministry. The selectors are looking for evidence that their self-assessment is valid: the church has to check out that their sense of call is echoed by the wider Church. There also needs to be evidence that they have the qualities needed. For instance, all professional ministries require the exercising of leadership and authority. Is there evidence of this capacity? Otherwise candidates may well be mistaken in understanding their call, however strong it seems to be. There will always be a mixture of inner and outward evidence that God is calling someone to ordained or accredited lay ministry.

9

Frailty and Renewal

The treasure is in clay jars. The frailty of Christian leaders is a source of constant concern in churches today. Serious dangers lie in wait which can damage and even destroy Christian ministry. However, the grave warnings of this chapter must not lead the reader to think that Christian leadership is all doom and gloom. There are the most wonderful encouragements and joys, privileges and opportunities.

Many Christian leaders down the centuries rejoice to echo Paul's words to the Philippians 'I thank my God every time I remember you. In all my prayers for all of you, I always pray with *joy* because of your partnership in the gospel from the first day until now, being confident of this, that he who began a good work in you will carry it on to completion until the day of Christ Jesus' (Philippians 1.3-6; author's emphasis). And even when writing to the Church of Corinth with its many and serious problems, he wrote 'I always thank God for you because of his grace given you in Christ Jesus' (1 Corinthians 1.4).

Paul experienced some very tough times, but still said 'Since through God's mercy we have this ministry, we do not lose heart' and again 'we have this treasure in jars of clay to show that this all-surpassing power is from God and not from us' (2 Corinthians 4.1,7). But the dangers are real, and have a long history. They are, in fact, nothing new.

Frail leaders

Consider the frailties of great leaders in Old Testament times. Abraham – unbelieving, argumentative, deceitful; Moses – arrogant, argumentative, disobedient, workaholic; Elijah – fearful, neurotic, depressive. There are, of course, plenty more examples – with King David another outstanding candidate.

Jesus' disciples showed great frailty in the Gospel accounts – slow to understand, to believe and to obey, they lacked humility, and faithfulness in

93

adversity. The Early Church was marked by very real frailties and the leadership shared in these and often took some time to take the appropriate steps required. There were bitter misunderstandings and disputes about mission policy towards Gentiles, and about selection of staff colleagues (Acts 15.36-41). Problems at Ephesus (see Acts 20.29-31), at Corinth and in the churches John addressed in Asia Minor (Revelation 2 and 3) clearly involved leadership problems as well as other issues.

Similar problems occur today – in all churches, old and new. Some Christians think the grass is greener in another part of the field. A knowledge of church history and a more than superficial understanding of different churches today (including those who frequently criticize others) show that frailties with regard to:

> orthodoxy in teaching
>
> morality in behaviour

and

> humility in ministry

are endemic issues in all kinds of churches. Let those who think they stand firm take heed lest they fall!

When things go wrong in Christian leadership, what should be done?

Christian response

Too frequently Christians have leaped to judgement, gossip, criticism, condemnation, division and schism. The Scriptures urge us to be much more cautious, measured, humble and gentle. Some Christians immediately jump to issues of discipline. However, the Bible indicates a whole series of important dimensions which can prevent, reduce or repair the serious consequences of human frailty in leadership. Consider:

1.   *Shared* leadership rather than one-person leadership will avoid many dangers (see Chapter 7, and page 98 later in this chapter).

2.   *Prayer* for leaders needs to be taught, modelled, valued and constantly practised. Before criticism of leaders is ever ventured, it would be an excellent discipline to consider how much we have prayed for them.

3.   *Care* for leaders. They are to be respected and held 'in the highest regard in love' because of their work (1 Thessalonians 5.13). The question is more often asked nowadays 'who cares for the carers?' or

'who pastors the pastor?' Many Christian churches have systems of oversight (*episcope*) beyond the local church or parish. The Church of England has bishops and archdeacons, the Roman Catholics have bishops, the Methodists have area chairmen, the United Reformed Church has provincial moderators and the Baptists have superintendents. An important aspect of the work of these senior diocesan/regional/district leaders is to exercise a pastoral care/oversight of clergy/ministers/pastors. However, the responsibilities of such senior leaders are often such that they would have only occasional contact with local leaders. Thus care for parish/local church leaders must be primarily sought in the mutual life of a local shared leadership and/or the systematic care given by senior lay members. (For the story of Moses and Jethro, see Chapter 7, pages 80f.)

4. *Teaching* of leaders. It is all too possible for leaders to give out so much, but not to be adequately refuelled themselves; to teach so much, but to rely on their own ordination or other training which may be many years past. It is quite possible for a leader to be in error about a particular matter. There is an interesting example in Acts 18.25-26. Apollos 'began to speak boldly in the synagogue . . . he spoke with great fervour and taught about Jesus accurately, though he knew only the baptism of John . . . . When Priscilla and Aquila heard him, they invited him to their home and explained to him the way of God more adequately.' This is a ministry perhaps undertaken too infrequently nowadays. It needs both theological knowledge and a very gentle, winsome spirit. Private and discreet tuition is the pattern here rather than public criticism (or megaphone diplomacy). Nowadays, writing of books and articles plays an important role.

5. *Dialogue and controversy* have a place too. It is when the arguments are associated with a failure to listen, to be courteous and to be honest that they have a bad reputation and are counter-productive. There is much dialogue and controversy in the Bible from the prophets, through Jesus' debates with Pharisees and Saduccees, to Paul and other New Testament letter-writers who argue with church congregations to bring them to a better mind on issues of doctrine, morality, unity, humility, and other features of church and community life.

Readers will note that the categories are developing but we have still not reached disciplinary procedures. There is one other category to be considered before that.

6.   (Early) *retirement* or severance. Some serious problems develop with leaders because of their age, or because they have been too long in a particular place or appointment. Some have grown weary – physically, mentally, emotionally or spiritually. Churches need careful systems not only of appointment to offices of leadership but also of review, of termination, of transfer and/or of (early) retirement or severance. If we don't have such a system, then problem situations fester and grow to become very big issues which gravely damage church life.

7.   *Disciplinary* procedures. These are matters of last (not first) resort. Has there been sharing, prayer, care, teaching, dialogue and careful enquiry into retirement/transfer possibilities? Discipline is an unpleasant concept to many because they associate it with harshness, narrowness and bigotry. But note Paul's words 'if someone is caught in a sin, you who are spiritual should restore that person gently. But watch yourself, or you also may be tempted' (Galatians 6.1). Discipline is to be conducted:

- by those who are spiritual – mature;
- where the evidence is very clear – 'caught in a sin';
- in a gentle fashion – never harsh;
- with a view to restoration;
- with immense care by the leaders about their own spiritual position.

There are Early Church references to possibilities of expulsion or excommunication in extreme situations (i.e. Matthew 18.15-17; 1 Corinthians 5).

It is not unknown to hear appeals for more discipline in the churches today. We need to add two caveats. Firstly, we need much more of the earlier dimensions listed as a Christian response to leadership frailty. If we get these more thoroughly in place, the discipline issues will be considered in a much better context. Secondly, the prurience and inaccuracies of the national press make public church discipline very problematical today. This is part of the reason why much discipline of Christian leaders happens in a semi-private and more informal way. This has its own dangers of injustice and grievance. The issue is thoroughly addressed in the recent report *Under Authority – Report on Church Discipline*.[1] This report includes recommendations for major reform of the Church of England's disciplinary procedures. Legislation to this end is in preparation.

Dangers for leaders

These can come from outside of us and from within and, indeed, from a combination of external and internal factors. Some of the most serious dangers are:

Drifting away from God – or, rather, from a conscious awareness of the living presence of God in daily life

Christian leaders, like everyone else, should heed the words 'Seek the Lord while he may be found' (Isaiah 55.6) and, 'Come near to God and he will come near to you' (James 4.8) and 'Do not put out the Spirit's fire' (1 Thessalonians 5.19). But an ignoring of these appeals is all too possible for clergy and other Christian leaders. In fact, they are prone to particular temptation and vulnerability here. Because they work so constantly and 'professionally' with Scripture, with sacraments and with pastoral care, it can all become a mere habit, a chore even. Then gradually, imperceptibly, a loss of zeal for the gospel, the kingdom of God and service to others creeps upon us. Prayer can become a ritual with little sense of reality let alone joy.

What is to be done? As with all the dangers considered here – prevention is better than cure. This is not a specialist study[2] in these issues, but some pointers will be suggested both to avoid the dangers and, sometimes, to escape from them.

With respect to this particular danger consider:

- spiritual disciplines of regular [daily] worship which include prayer and Scripture which nourish the heart and soul and which include the regular [weekly] participation in Holy Communion;

- spiritual direction – regular meeting with a soul-friend who will encourage, exhort and pray;

- retreat – a regular (at least annual) time alone with God. Some days (or even hours) when we deliberately and decisively leave our normal lifestyle and setting, and devote ourselves to seeking God and his way for our lives. Fasting can be an important aspect of this discipline;

- renewal – there are many types and dimensions of spiritual renewal. We need to know about them. They have often been oases in deserts, lights in dark places and paths back to a real knowledge of God.

Loneliness, disappointment and discouragement

There are certain warning signals that indicate this group of dangers. The 'them – and – us' syndrome is a clear indicator, but often unrecognized. Note how clergy or leaders may return from a church service, meeting or other event and say something like *'they* weren't in very good form today' or *'they* made a mess of that discussion or decision'. It is the pronoun *they* that indicates that the leader is distancing him/herself from others in the congregation or group.

This distancing, or retreat from identification with the church or group, is a warning signal about loneliness – actual or potential. It is often linked to disappointment or discouragement. When things are encouraging, leaders will normally use the pronoun *we*, e.g. *we* had a good service, or meeting, etc.

This situation can develop into the 'Elijah-complex' – 'I am the only one left' (1 Kings 19.14). This is often a neurotic reaction where a leader simply fails to recognize and value others who are on the same side and will be supportive in difficult situations. Many clergy and leaders can be lonely in their church or parish, or fail to have good relationships with neighbouring church leaders, or with their bishops or other senior leaders.

Actions to guard against these dangers will include:

- friendships within the church and beyond;
- shared leadership;
- spiritual direction.

Work and rest

Many Christian leaders find it very difficult to achieve a proper balance between work and rest. The large majority over-work, with the dangers of stress for themselves, their families and others, and exhaustion (see Chapter 7 and the case of Moses). There are also some who are disorganized and do not really work hard or effectively at all. It is very difficult to monitor this kind of work, and it is quite possible for clergy to waste their time or spend it doing inappropriate things. Many Christian leaders appear to be constantly overwhelmed by the pressure of their work, the pressure of and expectations from others or from themselves. Human beings were made to work but also to rest. We need both work and rest.[3]

To get the balance reasonably right, certain boundaries need to be carefully considered and then observed. The centuries-old tradition is that the clergy live in and work from a vicarage or similar tied-house. It is normally clearly identifiable and widely known. Some clergy increasingly use a church vestry or other church rooms for interviewing and church business. Some have developed a full-scale office in the church or hall. However, most still use the parson's house as a significant workplace. They need to think carefully about whether they will want (or need) a boundary to be observed (most of the time) between the private – home part of the house and the public – work part. Some vicarage design attempts to make these distinct and separable.[4]

When the minister 'works from home' there will usually be need of not only boundaries of space but also boundaries of time. The traditional parish ministry has sometimes been described as being available pastorally 'to all of the people all of time'. This might have been a meaningful vision in an eighteenth-century small village, but in a town or city in our time it can be seriously dangerous. The following factors are relevant:

●   Clergy clearly need daily time for rest, relaxation, meals and house-work, etc.

●   They need a weekly 'day off' (at the very least) and proper periods of holiday.

●   They need time for prayer, meditation, study, preparation and planning.

●   They need friends, and the opportunity to entertain and relax with family and friends.

●   Clergy will vary widely in terms of their domestic arrangements. Some will be alone, or have spouse, child(ren), parent(s), friend(s), or lodger(s), etc.

Sometimes (and in many situations frequently or even normally) there will be no one to answer the vicarage bell during many hours of the day or evening. Two principles seem clear:

Firstly, the pattern of Jesus' ministry (and other biblical material) does not exemplify nor require unbounded availability. Our Lord himself frequently sought solitude for quiet and prayer. He also gladly accepted invitations to parties and devoted special time to friends and colleagues.

Secondly, the 'when I'm at home I'm available' pattern is dangerous to personal health, marriage, family and friendships. There are too many stories of clergy saying that if they want some peace they have to 'go away' and 'get out of the vicarage'. This is an obvious recipe for stress-related illness.

Christian leaders need training for and discipline with respect to:

- managing time;

- managing administration. The often-drawn contrast between concern about people and paper is largely false. An efficient approach to letters, filing and planning (i.e. paperwork) can release a leader for more extensive time for pastoral care, leadership development and strategic thinking (i.e. people-work).

- managing priorities. This involves distinguishing the important and the urgent. It involves consideration of tools such as the SMART test for objectives or aims. Are they:

S	specific
M	measurable
A	agreed
R	realistic
T	time-bound?

When leaders conduct their ministries without some kind of strategic thinking and objectives, they can spend their time primarily reacting to whatever comes at them, whatever is on the top of the pile on the desk, and whichever is the loudest voice calling for attention. This is the way of stress and of reduced effectiveness.

Money

Leaders are not to be lovers of money (1 Timothy 3.3). This is a danger that can be a temptation at any time, but it can specially come to middle-aged and older people. The positive characteristic to develop in order to avoid this danger is contentment. Paul said 'I have learned to be content whatever the circumstances' (Philippians 4.11).

Clergy and other Christian leaders should have an appropriate stipend and pension (cf. 1 Timothy 5.17) which keeps them from anxiety, should have their working expenses properly reimbursed, and should have reasonable accommodation. Standards and expectations in all these areas have risen very significantly since the 1960s. The line between reasonable expectation and greed is not always easy to trace. Practical steps to avoid danger and temptation in this area are:

- obtain receipts for all working expenses and keep a proper duplicate book;

- never handle church cash (unless absolutely unavoidable);

- do not be a signatory for church cheques;

- if you have to be a signatory, never sign blank cheques;

- make sure *all* accounts are treated properly and are audited;

- if you are in, or get into, debt – seek professional help *immediately* (from a senior Christian leader, experienced accountant or bank manager).

Sex and marriage

Grave dangers for Christian leaders are in these areas of life. The Bible commends either unmarried celibacy or faithful marriage of husband and wife. The Church of England bishops re-stated that position for Christian leaders in their report *Issues in Human Sexuality*.[5] Virtually all other churches support that position. Sexuality is given by God. It is important, it is good, but it is powerful and dangerous.

Clergy and other Christian leaders have special responsibility and reason to have both clear convictions and strong discipline in these areas. In their ministries they will inevitably be involved with people who are trusting and vulnerable – the young, the distressed, the widowed, the emotional. Many fine and promising ministries have been damaged or even ruined beyond repair by frailty here. In addition, the situations of those who have sought Christian counsel have been made worse.

What is to be done?

- Keep your theological and ethical convictions clear and strong in these areas.

- Be gentle and affectionate to all, but with very clear boundaries in personal and pastoral relationships.

- Have plenty of (or at least several) good friends of both sexes.

- Be very clear about the dangers and inappropriateness of being alone with people in emotional circumstances and late at night.

- Be constantly watchful of yourself, your actions and motives and how they can be understood or misunderstood by others. Also we need to be watchful of others – temptation, obsession and seduction can come from others as well as from within ourselves.

- Those who are married need to work hard and realistically to keep the marriage in a healthy and joyful state.

- If you get into real difficulties, seek for appropriate help (e.g. from Relate – the marriage and relationships counselling organization) – usually the quicker the better!

- Keep well away from pornography in its various forms, and be realistic about the effects of erotic literature and films.

Alcohol

Wine gladdens the heart (Psalm 104.15) but the warnings about its dangers are frequent in the Bible (e.g. 1 Timothy 3.3), in history and in daily experience. Unfortunately, people who drink too much are strongly prone to deny they have any problem, and increasingly become devious and deceitful.

The words of advice from one organization which helps people in this area are the HALT guidelines. These warn us to be particularly alert to the dangers of alcoholic drinking when:

H   hungry

A   angry

L   lonely

T   tired

If you detect problems or if anyone else raises a question about your drinking, seek expert advice immediately (from your medical doctor or from one of the specialist organizations such as Al Anon, Alcoholics Anonymous or the National Alcohol Helpline 'Drinkline'). Again, honest friends and a good spiritual director could enable the problem to be faced and help found.

Anger and relationships

Uncontrolled anger and quarrelsome bad-tempered relationships also damage and destroy Christian ministry. We have seen that Christian leaders are to be 'temperate, self-controlled, not violent, not quarrelsome' (1 Timothy 3.2,3) but, on the contrary, the fruit of the Spirit is 'love, joy, peace, patience, kindness, goodness, faithfulness, gentleness and self-control' (Galatians 5.22-

23). When harsh words have been spoken in privacy to one or two others, there is the possibility of repentance, apology and reconciliation. However, when there has been an outburst of uncontrolled anger and harsh words in a public situation, the difficulties in putting such a situation to rights are very substantial. It is like trying to clear up confetti in a gale-force wind. The damage done can be almost irreparable and confidence in the leadership damaged permanently. We need to take the utmost care to prevent such an episode. Once again, safeguards will include:

● shared leadership;

● spiritual direction;

● almost certainly, such behaviour will have its roots in one or more of the dangers already considered. This needs careful investigation and remedial attention – probably with the help of a professional counsellor.

Personal violence [6]

A survey of 21 stipendiary parochial clergy in an East London deanery in March/April 1997 revealed that 80 per cent of them had experienced their homes broken into and that 70 per cent had been assaulted or threatened in the course of their ministry. In an increasingly violent society it is therefore clear that issues of clergy safety need to be addressed. The pattern of clergy working alone, often living and working in isolated buildings endangers not only themselves but also those who live and work with them.

The parochial clergy are normally visible and public figures – easily identifiable and found in their communities. They not only frequently work from home, church or hall, but are out and about in the streets, homes, hospitals, hostels and just about anywhere in their parish. Clergy also work very irregular hours – frequently evenings, and occasionally late into the night. Situations and factors of particular significance are:

● alcohol and drug abuse;

● involvement with domestic violence;

● the aggressive request/demand for money or assistance;

● the mentally ill;

● those living rough.

Christian ministry is specially available for those in need, and Christian leaders will wish to be hospitable (2 Timothy 3.2).

However, safety from personal violence will require careful consideration of the boundaries of space and time already mentioned on page 99f. Appropriate training, working in teams and careful review are important. In addition, Christian leaders need to be realistic about their skills, and not go into situations or attempt to help people with problems well beyond their knowledge, experience, skills and resources.

There are grave dangers and temptations that lie in wait for the Christian leader. They are ignored at our peril. Forewarned is to be (hopefully) fore-armed. We are called to 'be strong in the Lord and in his mighty power . . . .our struggle is not against flesh and blood . . . but against the spiritual forces of evil . . . Therefore put on the full armour of God, so that when the day of evil comes, you may be able to stand your ground . . . put on truth, righteousness, the gospel of peace, faith, salvation, the word of God . . . and pray in the Spirit' (Ephesians 6.10-18).

The hymn St Patrick's Breastplate can be used as such a prayer:

I bind myself to God today,
the strong and holy Trinity,
to know his name and make him known,
the Three-in-One and One-in-Three.

I bind myself to God for ever,
to Jesus in his incarnation,
baptized for me in Jordan river
and crucified for my salvation;
he burst the prison of his tomb,
ascended to the heavenly throne,
returning at the day of doom;
by faith I make his life my own.

I *bind myself to God today,*
to his great power to hold and lead,
his eye to watch me on my way,
his ear to listen to my need;
the wisdom of my God to teach,
his hand to guide, his shield to ward,
the word of God to give me speech,
his heavenly host to be my guard.

Christ be with me, Christ within me,
Christ behind me, Christ before me,
Christ to seek me, Christ to win me,
Christ to comfort and restore me;
Christ beneath me, Christ above me,
Christ in quiet, Christ in danger,
Christ sustaining all who love me,
Christ uniting friend and stranger.

I *bind myself to God today,*
the strong and holy Trinity,
to know his name and make him known,
the Three-in-One and One-in-Three;
from him all nature has creation,
eternal Father, Spirit, Word:
praise God, my strength and my salvation!
Praise in the Spirit through Christ the Lord. Amen.

(after Patrick (*c.* 385 – 461))
Cecil F. Alexander (1818 – 95)
© in this version *Jubilate Hymns*

Renewal

We may well have sung –

> O Jesus I have promised
>
> To serve you to the end.

or

> Jesus is Lord!

But clergy and other Christian leaders will be (or should be) aware of their flawed obedience. The story of the disciple/apostle Simon Peter is surely a supreme example of vocation and frailty, inconsistency and failure – and yet of forgiveness and reinstatement.

Read John chapter 21 – and note:

1. The *history* – of Peter's inconsistency. He recognized and confessed the Messiahship of Jesus, but then tried to stop him pursuing that vocation as a suffering servant. He could not bear the idea of Jesus washing his feet, but then wanted hands and head bathed as well. He said he would die for Jesus, and then denied he knew him (Mark 8.27-33; John 13.6-10,37; 18.15-18, 25-27).

Peter (named *petros*, rock, but so impulsive and unreliable) is now face-to-face with the risen Christ – a tense and dramatic situation.

2. The *reminder*. The story of the failed fishing trip followed by directions from Jesus and remarkable success is a reminder of a previous episode – recounted in Luke 5.1-11. The reminder was a means of grace to a shattered and downcast soul. The liturgy, the Scripture, the sacraments and the church are all means of grace – reminders of God's action in the past and character in the present. 'Do this in remembrance of me' (1 Corinthians 11.24,25).

As well as a reminder of a previous episode, it was surely a reminder of Jesus' earlier commission 'From now on you will catch men and women' – rather than fish (Luke 5.10). There is nothing wrong with fishing (earning a living by one's skills) but in Peter's case Jesus called him to be an evangelist and apostle.

3. The *meal* – Jesus had prepared a barbecue on the beach. It was a reminder of many meals together in earlier days – with their friendship, sharing and teaching. It was a sign of Jesus' thoughtful care after the night of weary and frustrating toil. There is a considerable pastoral significance in such thoughtful care, hospitality, visiting and having meals together. People need to know that we care, before they care about what we know.

4. The *questions* are not explicitly about knowledge, or service, or faithfulness – although there are implicit elements of all these. The questions are focused explicitly on *love* for Jesus Christ – 'Do you love me?' That love is the supreme issue should come as no surprise. The great commandment is to *love* God with all our heart, mind, strength and soul – and to *love* our neighbour as ourself. (Matthew 22.37ff. quoting Deuteronomy 6.5 and Leviticus 19.18). Jesus told his followers that it was through their *love* they would be recognized as his disciples (John 13.34ff.). Paul said 'And now these three remain: faith, hope and love. But the greatest of these is *love*.' (1 Corinthians 13.13; author's emphasis).

These questions about love are not a matter of mere sentiment or emotion. The first question 'Do you truly love me *more than these*?' might be referring to the other disciples, i.e. do you really think you are superior to your colleagues? A challenge to pride – which is a real peril in ministry. Again, the questions are phrased 'do you truly love *me*?' Is Jesus requiring Peter not only to acknowledge and love a Messiah but a suffering servant whose vocation he once attempted to thwart? Then again, Jesus asked a *third* time. No wonder (v.17) Peter was hurt because Jesus asked him a *third* time. Surely it was an obvious recalling of the threefold denial.

The questions of the Lord, the questions about love are probing and can be painful. Just as a wound may need to be re-opened in order to be cleaned before true healing can take place, and a leg may need painful straightening after a break. Here is something of the painful role of the pastor, the spiritual director, the true soul friend.

5. The *re-commissioning* – Many would be tempted to give up on Simon Peter. But here is the grace and insight of forgiveness, healing and re-instatement. In this chapter we have looked at the frailties of Christian ministers/leaders and the serious dangers and temptations that can assail them and bring shipwreck to their ministry. But foundational to the ministry of Jesus is salvation/rescue from sin, despair and spiritual weakness. He brings forgiveness, healing, the opportunity to turn around (repentance and conversion), start again (new birth, regeneration) and have a new dynamic through his Holy Spirit.

Peter is re-commissioned to be a shepherd, a pastor. 'Feed my lambs' – the vulnerable ones who are hungry (for spiritual truth), harassed (by so many conflicting pressures) and helpless (without divine power). 'Take care of my sheep' – the maturing people of God who need equipping to be effective disciples, servants and envoys for the kingdom. And, at the end, re-commissioned – for martyrdom (vv.18ff)!

There are certainly many dangers for Christian leaders. Their weaknesses and failures can have very serious effects on their churches and on other people. But the God of all mercy is long-suffering and of great goodness. He loves to restore, to forgive and to renew. Thanks to God!

The ASB Collect for Ash Wednesday

> *Almighty and everlasting God,*
> *you hate nothing that you have made*
> *and forgive the sins of all those who are penitent.*
> *Create and make in us new and contrite hearts,*
> *that, lamenting our sins*
> > *and acknowledging our wretchedness,*
> *we may receive from you, the God of all mercy,*
> *perfect forgiveness and peace;*
> *through Jesus Christ our Lord.*

ASB Collect for Lent 1

> *Almighty God,*
> *whose Son Jesus Christ fasted forty days in the wilderness,*
> *and was tempted as we are, yet without sin:*
> *give us grace to discipline ourselves*
> > *in obedience to your Spirit;*
> *and, as you know our weakness,*
> *so may we know your power to save;*
> *through Jesus Christ our Lord.*

ASB Collects for Pentecost

Almighty God,
who at this time
taught the hearts of your faithful people
by sending to them the light of your Holy Spirit:
grant us by the same Spirit
to have a right judgement in all things,
and evermore to rejoice in his holy comfort;
through the merits of Christ Jesus our Saviour,
who is alive and reigns with you in the unity of the Spirit,
one God, now and for ever.

Almighty God,
who on the day of Pentecost
sent your Holy Spirit to the disciples
with the wind from heaven in tongues of flame,
filling them with joy
and boldness to preach the Gospel:
send us out in the power of the same Spirit
to witness to your truth
and to draw everyone to the fire of your love;
through Jesus Christ our Lord.

Appendix: A Good Minister

This is the text of a sermon (slightly edited for publication). A few sentences and references have already been used in the main text of the book, but have still been retained.

1 Timothy 4.6-16

> If you point these things out to the brothers and sisters, you will be a good minister of Christ Jesus, brought up in the truths of the faith and of the good teaching that you have followed. [7]Have nothing to do with godless myths and old wives' tales; rather, train yourself to be godly. [8]For physical training is of some value, but godliness has value for all things, holding promise for both the present life and the life to come. [9]This is a trustworthy saying that deserves full acceptance [10](and for this we labour and strive), that we have put our hope in the living God, who is the Saviour of all people, and especially of those who believe. [11]Command and teach these things. [12]Don't let anyone look down on you because you are young, but set an example to the believers in speech, in life, in love, in faith and in purity. [13]Until I come, devote yourself to the public reading of Scripture, to preaching and to teaching. [14]Do not neglect your gift, which was given you through a prophetic message when the body of elders laid their hands on you. [15]Be diligent in these matters; give yourself wholly to them, so that everyone may see your progress. [16]Watch your life and doctrine closely. Persevere in them, because if you do, you will save both yourself and your hearers.

Introduction

There has been a hi-jack. You know how when we hear about that on the news, about an airliner or a building, how pleased we are when some people are set free. Sometimes the hi-jackers let large groups of people free. They just keep a few people prisoner, and we pray, don't we, that everyone will be set free? One of the most exciting things about the last 30 years that I have been ordained is that a lot of people have been set free from this particular hi-jack. It is 'ministry' that has been hi-jacked. Through hundreds of years, in every continent, in virtually every church, ministry has been hi-jacked by the clergy, and the lay people have gone along with it. Have you heard it said of someone – 'She's going into the ministry', because she/he is going to a theological college to train to be ordained? 'Going into the ministry' – as if ordination and turning your collar round is 'the ministry'. Does the Bible ever talk like that? Never. What the Bible says is that all Christian people, the whole Church of God, are called to ministry. When we are baptized, when we put our faith in Jesus Christ, we are called to be ministers or servants of God. What has happened, especially over the last 30 years in Britain, is that large numbers of Christian people have been released from this hi-jack. Many of the clergy have started to see things very differently and thousands of the lay people have as well. So churches can be roughly in one of three situations:

1. The old position that I can remember from when I was a child was that the vicar was *the* minister. So what did the lay people do? They received his ministry of word and sacrament and pastoral care.

2. There were some 'keen' churches where people said, 'The vicar can't do it all on his own.' So the keen lay people 'helped the vicar in his ministry'. Many keen people ran the Sunday Schools and looked after the buildings and the finances and many other things. But if you asked them why they were doing this, they would say, 'I am helping the vicar in his ministry.'

3. But more and more there is a third way in which churches can live that turns the first position absolutely upside down, where it is realized that *all* God's people are called to the ministry to serve God. That is what the word 'ministry' means – not just in church, on Sundays, or in home groups during the week but, in actual fact, called to serve God every day of the week, in factories and offices, and schools and universities, and at home, and out in the community. We are called to serve God all the time. So what is the role of the clergy? Can they pack up? Not at all. Their job is a distinctive and particular ministry. It is to equip the people to serve God, day by day. To equip the whole people of God in their ministry. That is what the New Testament teaches. That has become more and more widely understood over the last 30 years. More and more people are set free from the hi-jack. My great longing is to see in the next few years the whole Church of England set free from this hi-jack. So that in every parish, the whole people of God are exercising their ministry and the clergy are equipping them to do it. That's what I long for!

Now although we are all called to ministry, some people within that ministry are called to *leadership*. Some of them are ordained leaders and some lay leaders. So the church wardens are called to lay leadership and so are home group leaders. Youth leaders are called to lay leadership. Readers are lay leaders. So we are not just thinking about the ordained leaders, but about all the leaders. This letter to the young leader Timothy teaches about leadership in God's Church. We are all interested in leadership, aren't we? Leadership in the country, leadership in the monarchy, leadership in the government, leadership in the schools, leadership in the police force. What about leadership in the Church? Turn to 1 Timothy 4 verse 6. The author has been talking about the problems of false teaching and Timothy handling it, and he then says, 'If you point these things out to the brothers you will be a good *minister.*' And then what does it say? 'A good minister of St John's or Christ Church or of the Church of England'? – not at all! Firstly a good minister of *Jesus Christ!*

A minister of Jesus Christ

Some people complain about how some ordinands get through the selection system. Sometimes I say to them 'there is one great problem about choosing the new clergy, we only have the laity to choose from!' We get the leadership we deserve. The higher the spiritual quality of the lay people in our church, the higher will be the spiritual quality of our leaders. So this sermon is about leadership, but it is really for all of you, including the young people. You may not be a leader now, but God may call you in five or ten years' time. The first thing is that we are called to be good ministers of Jesus. I don't know what you're facing tomorrow – your office, your factory, a hard day's work at home, volunteer work in the community, school, university, whatever it is, but if you go off tomorrow morning, thinking 'today I am a minister for Jesus', will that make a difference? It does to me. Today, not first and foremost, a minister of the Church of England, or even of the Church of God, but, today, I am going to serve Jesus. Now how are we going to be good servants of Jesus this coming week?

Proper diet

I wonder whether you grew up with a parent or a guardian who said to you, 'You must have a proper breakfast.' We need a good diet, and parents and guardians give careful attention, don't they, to what children eat? Look at verse 6b, 'a good minister of Jesus Christ brought up (the Greek word means nourished, fed) in the truths of the faith and of the good teaching that you followed'. I recently became a granddad – to twins. I had forgotten how careful you have to be about the milk, and about gradually bringing them onto solids, so I am re-learning all this. Have you thought about the people who have the responsibility for the diet of your church? Sunday services, the home groups, those who are responsible for the diet of the Sunday School groups, Pathfinders, whatever you have. That's a great responsibility. Just as young parents have this enormous responsibility of feeding the little babies and the toddlers and the children in a way so they will grow up strong. It is the same responsibility that your vicar and his/her associate leaders have to feed you. You are all at different levels, it is a very demanding exercise. Some of you have been walking with God for 50 years, some of you are toddlers, some of you are just finding your way to faith. To teach you and nurture you is a very demanding task but it is very important. To nourish you in the faith! That is the first thing. If we are going to be good ministers of Jesus Christ, we need a good diet that will be nourishing.

Good discipline

Look at verse 7b: 'train yourself to be godly.' I wonder how many of you take regular exercise. You may play badminton, or golf, or you walk the dog, or you have an exercise bike. People put a lot of thought into keeping fit! Sometimes there is a strange noise coming from our living room and I am supposed to keep out of the way, because my wife is with Rosemary Conley! She has the fitness video on the television. People take a lot of care over keeping physically fit. Do we give anywhere near as much attention to keeping spiritually fit? 'Train yourself to be godly. For physical training is of some value.' God gave us our bodies and we are to look after them for Him. 'But godliness has value for all things, both for the present life and the life to come.' So how can we keep spiritually fit? What kind of training system?

Swimming is my thing and when I am on holiday I swim often several times a day. But when I am not on holiday I just don't get round to it. And, of course, to keep fit through swimming you have to swim at least twice a week. So I am a 'fits and starts man' when it comes to keeping fit. There are many Christians who are 'fits and starts people'. They go off to Spring Harvest, or some kind of Christian convention or retreat and they get a spiritual injection. Then they come back and get so involved in the busyness of life and forget the training. You don't keep fit that way. We need some discipline about how we read the Bible, how we pray, how we worship, and how we serve God. I am so grateful for those who introduced me to the idea of having a spiritual director and of going on retreat once or twice a year, to be absolutely alone with God, to be quiet with him. These are aspects of a discipline.

We need a proper diet, we need a proper discipline or training.

Hard work

If we are going to be ministers for Jesus, it is going to involve hard work. It is not going to be easy. Look at verse 9: 'This is a trustworthy saying that deserves full acceptance (and for this we *labour* and *strive*), that we put our hope in the living God, who is the Saviour.' If we really believe God is the living God, if we really believe that Jesus is the saviour, we will roll up our sleeves and do something about it. You can't just be an armchair kind of person, or someone who stands on the touchline and cheers the others along, you are going to be a player on the pitch. We are going to be labouring. The first Greek word is 'toil', weary toil, and the second word 'strive' is the Greek word *agonizo* 'to agonize'. If we are to be involved in Christian service and leadership there will be times of agonizing, when we weep tears of perplexity – 'Why is my witness not more effective? Why are the people I teach in Sunday School or in the home group I lead not more responsive? Why are there not more signs?'

Do you remember how perplexed Jesus was with the disciples? And he was the Son of God, he was the best teacher in the world. Do you remember how often he said to them, 'Why are you so thick?' (That is my translation!) Jesus could not understand why they did not understand his patient, clear teaching about who he was and about why he had come, to die as the saviour of the world. They wanted to make him a king, and take over the Roman Empire. And they had got it all wrong because they did not understand. They did not have the spiritual perception. Agonizing!

Leadership in the Christian Church is not easy today in England. Many of the bishops agonize about their work, and the clergy and lay leaders are often in anguish about their work. 'Why isn't God doing more in our country, in our parish, in our diocese?'

So we are called to be good ministers for Jesus Christ.

But there are some people who are very eager to be good servants of Jesus but they have a problem. They just don't get on with *other people*! There are some with great ideas about serving God, but just don't get on with others. Jesus had that problem with the disciples. Do you remember that after they had walked through the muddy streets of Jerusalem on that last night they were together and they went to the upper room? All the disciples looked at one another and – were they thinking 'why shouldn't *he* wash feet because he is younger than me?' Or 'why shouldn't *he* wash feet because he is not as important as me?' Weren't they upset when Jesus got up first and took the water and washed their feet? Peter was so distressed about it, he said, 'No

Lord, please don't do it!' And when Jesus sat down again afterwards, he said to the disciples, 'What I have done for you, you must do for each other.' It is one thing being a minister for Jesus – that sounds very holy and pious. But it is quite another thing washing the feet of your next door neighbour or that awkward person in your church, your home group or on the PCC. That is another thing.

So we must also be a minister of others.

A minister of others

Look at verse 11: 'Command and teach these things.' Verse 12 says, 'Don't let anyone look down on you because you are young.' Now that word means people under 40. We unequivocally need *young* people in leadership. Don't let anyone look down on you because you are young. We need *young* leaders in the Church of England. We want the older people as well, but we want *young* people in leadership in the parishes and in the dioceses and in the church nationally. But how are we going to be servants of *people* as well as being servants of Jesus?

An example

The first thing is 'set an *example* for the believers' (v.12b; author's emphasis). We have a saying – 'Actions speak louder than words.' They do, don't they? When I think of the Sunday School teachers I had, 40 to 50 years ago, I can't remember much of what they actually *said*, but I can remember what they were *like*. I can remember their kindness, I can remember the interest they took, I can remember that they prayed for me. We need to be an example in the way we speak. One harsh word can undo a year of witness. Examples in the way we live, in the way we love people. That is what they will remember. It was said about the early Christians, 'Look how they love each other.' That is what struck the people round about. Is it what they say about your church? – 'They love each other.' And examples in the way we believe in Jesus and examples in purity! The world out there wants examples of unembarrassed holiness! Not just about sex, although that is important, but about money, and ambition, and home life, and relationships. Examples of unembarrassed holiness! Purity! Not people who show off about it, but people who just quietly live it. The philosopher, Nietzsche, said to Christians, 'Show me you are redeemed, if you want me to believe in your redeemer.' That is fair enough. Someone else said, 'People want to know that we care, before they care about what we know.' So if we are going to serve others we must be an example.

Communication

But secondly if we are going to serve others we need to *communicate* appropriately. Look at verse 13: 'Until I come, devote yourself to the public reading of Scripture, to preaching and to teaching.' In other words, preach the good news and teach people about God's will. Now this is a very demanding business. Sometimes people say, 'Why should ordinands spend three years at theological college and why do we need £8 million a year to train 1,200 ordinands?' Well partly because it is very demanding to communicate Christian faith appropriately today.

There are many kinds of preaching. I had a two-page spread in Women's Own about the problems of the vicar in 'EastEnders' and preached to more people in those two pages than in a whole year from pulpits. Then, of course, there is preaching on Sunday and there is leading a school assembly. Then there is preaching in a prison, that is different again, and then there is preaching at a funeral. That is the sort of thing your vicar is doing, week in and week out. Then there are the people who stop you in the road and expect you to give an answer in less than a minute on some profound question. I went into a primary school when I was a young vicar and the teacher said, 'This is the new vicar, have you got any questions?' A little five-year-old girl put her hand up and said, 'What is God like?' I said, 'God is like Jesus' and having seen on the classroom bookshelf the Ladybird book on the stories of Jesus I added, 'If you want to know about God, learn about Jesus, because he came to tell us about God, to show us God.' It may not be the whole truth but we have to be able to speak true truths to little children. Preaching and teaching in all these different situations is very demanding.

There was a curate who was very nervous about his first sermon. He met the vicar down the High Street. 'What *shall* I preach about on Sunday?' The old vicar said 'About God, and about ten minutes!' I was brought up in South India where if you preach for less than an hour they think there is something wrong! But we do need, whatever their length, sermons and talks that will nourish us for today. We need them to help us walk with God today and during the coming week. Not many of the sermons will be spectacular, published, in neon lights, but the test of a sermon is – 'Does it nourish people today?' Does it tell them about God, and about his will for today? And then they come back again because they want more. We don't just eat once a month do we? So we come back regularly to be nourished with the word of God. This is a very demanding ministry for others.

Perseverance

If we are to be ministers for others, we must be not only an example, not only appropriate communicators but we must be people who are going to go on! *Persevere!* Look at verse 14: 'Do not neglect your gift' and there is a reference to ordination there, right in the first century. Verse 15 says, 'Be diligent' and verse 16 says, 'Watch your life and doctrine closely. *Persevere* in them' (author's emphasis). We need leaders who are going to persevere through thick and thin, and sometimes it will be very tough being a Christian leader in Britain today. We want people who are going to persevere!

God is looking for good ministers –

good ministers of Jesus Christ

and

good ministers of others.

Is he speaking to you?

Notes

Preface

1. Though as I complete this text, there is published Steven Croft, *Ministry in Three Dimensions* and Alastair Redfern, *Ministry and Priesthood*.

Chapter 1   Jesus – The Model

1. Introductory studies include:

   Graham N. Stanton, *The Gospels and Jesus*, Oxford University Press, 1989; Richard A. Burridge, *Four Gospels, One Jesus?*, SPCK, 1994; John Drane, *Jesus and the Four Gospels*, Lion, 1979; R. T. France, *The Man they Crucified*, IVP, 1975; C. H. Dodd, *The Founder of Christianity*, Collins, 1971.

2. The sacramental model of the Church is helpful at this point. The sacrament expresses both identity (fulfilment) and difference (promise) at the same time. See B. Horne and R. Hannaford in C. Hall and R. Hannaford (eds), *Order and Ministry*.

Chapter 2   Church and Ministry

1. See also Robert Hannaford, *Foundations for an Ecclesiology of Ministry* in C. Hall and R. Hannaford (eds), *Order and Ministry*.

2. N. Sykes, *Old Priest and New Presbyter*, CUP, 1956.

3. For another view on the meaning of the word, see Chapter 4 (pp.28–9).

4. E. Brunner, *The Misunderstanding of the Church*, Lutterworth, 1952, p. 50.

5. *Baptism, Eucharist and Ministry* (in future, cited as BEM).

Chapter 3   Discipleship for All

1. I have used material from Gordon W. Kuhrt, *Believing in Baptism*.

2. James Denney, *The Death of Christ*, fourth edition, 1903, p. 185.

3. Rudolph Schnackenburg quoted in G. R. Beasley Murray, *Baptism in the New Testament*, Eerdmans, 1962/1984, p. 272, n.3.

4. G. R. Beasley-Murray, *Baptism in the New Testament*, p. 273.

5. *One Lord, One Baptism*, World Council of Churches Commission on Faith and Order Paper, p. 22.

6. See *All Are Called* and *Called to New Life – The World of Lay Discipleship*.

7.   See Philip King, *Good News for a Suffering World*, and the many books noted at the end of each chapter.

Chapter 4   Leadership

1.   J. N. Collins, *Diakonia – Reinterpreting the Ancient Sources.*

2.   John R.W. Stott, *One People – Clergy and Laity in God's Church.*

3.   House of Bishops, *Issues in Human Sexuality.*

4.   *Issues in Human Sexuality*, 5.13, p. 44.

5.   *Issues in Human Sexuality*, 5.16, p. 45.

6.   John R.W. Stott, *I Believe in Preaching.*

7.   Karl Barth, *The Word of God and the Word of Man*, German edition 1928; Hodder and Stoughton, 1935 (Peter Smith, 1958), pp. 123-4.

8.   *The Dogmatic Constitution on Divine Revelation*, ch. 6 entitled 'Sacred Scripture in the Life of the Church' quoted in Walter M. Abbott (ed.), *The Documents of Vatican II*, Geoffrey Chapman, 1967, para. 23.

9.   A.M. Ramsey, *The Christian Priest Today*, p.7.

10. See John R.W. Stott, *The Preacher's Portrait.*

11. Karl Barth, *The Word of God and the Word of Man*, pp. 100-104, quoted in Stott, *I Believe in Preaching*, p. 149.

12. Most older English translations placed a comma after 'to prepare God's people' but most newer ones do not. The major commentaries discuss the issue at length.

13. A. M. Ramsey, *The Christian Priest Today*, p.14.

Chapter 5   Historical Developments

1.   See Avery Dulles, *Models of the Church.*

2.   The classic study is Andrew Walker, *Restoring the Kingdom.*

3.   *Eucharistic Presidency* – A Theological Statement by the House of Bishops. The document is a valuable resource on the theology of the Church, ministry and the Eucharist

4.   Ibid., para. 3.26 on p. 30.

5.   Ibid., para. 4.2 on p. 34.

6.   Ibid., para. 4.15 on p. 39.

7.   Ibid., para. 3.28 on p. 31.

8.   Ibid., para. 3.29 on p. 31.

Notes

9. BEM, p. 24.

10. BEM, p. 26 and Episcopal Ministry: The Report of the Archbishops' Group on the Episcopate.

11. See the report Deacons in the Ministry of the Church and Christine Hall (ed.), The Deacon's Ministry.

12. BEM, p. 25.

13. BEM, p. 23 para. 17.

14. Priesthood of the Ordained Ministry, para.142. The Report was subjected to extensive criticism both in reviews and in the General Synod debate in 1986 (Report of Proceedings Vol.17, No.3, pp.742ff.).

15. Priesthood of the Ordained Ministry, p. 102.

16. See e.g. K. E. Kirk(ed.), The Apostolic Ministry, Hodder and Stoughton, 1946; R. C. Moberley, Ministerial Priesthood; A. M. Ramsey, The Christian Priest Today; Alec Graham, Postscript in Michael Bowering (ed.), Priesthood Here and Now.

17. BEM, p.23, para. 17.

18. See Jean Tillard, What Priesthood Has the Ministry?

19. See Michael Green, Freed to Serve and Colin Buchanan, Is the Church of England Biblical?

20. Green, Freed to Serve, pp. 84f.

21. J. B. Lightfoot, The Christian Ministry, p. 134 (Thynne and Jarvis).

22. Ministry Division, Statistics of Licensed Ministers.

23. See Nigel Peyton, Dual-Role Ministry.

24. Giles Legood (ed.), Chaplaincy — the Church's Sector Ministries.

25. See Ministry Division, Regulations for Non-Stipendiary Ministry; J. M. Francis and L.F. Francis (eds), Tentmaking — Perspectives on Self-Supporting Ministry; John Fuller and Patrick Vaughan (eds), Working for the Kingdom — The Story of Ministers in Secular Employment; P. Baelz and W. Jacob (eds), Ministers of the Kingdom — Exploration in Non-Stipendiary Ministry; Mark Hodge, Non-Stipendiary Ministry in the Church of England.

26. Ministry Division, Stranger in the Wings — A Report on Local Non-Stipendiary Ministry.

27. T. G. King, Readers: a Pioneer Ministry; Rhoda Hiscox, Celebrating Reader Ministry; Robert Martineau, The Office and Work of a Reader.

28. See Good News People — Recognizing Diocesan Evangelists.

29. See John Tiller, A Strategy for the Church's Ministry and Ministry Division, Shaping Ministry for a Missionary Church — A Review of Diocesan Ministry Strategy Documents.

Chapter 6   Women – In Leadership

1. See James B. Hurley, *Man and Woman in Biblical Perspective*.

2. See Elaine Storkey, *What's Right with Feminism?*; Rosie Nixson, *Liberating Women for the Gospel*; Elaine Storkey and Margaret Hebblethwaite, *Conversations on Christian Feminism* and the extensive literature cited in them.

3. See *The Ordination of Women to the Priesthood* – (A Second Report by the House of Bishops) also A *Digest* (of the above Report) for a thorough discussion of the main issues.

4. See the comments on 'the representative dimension of ministry' (p. 51) and on ministerial priesthood in Chapter 5.

5. In the Papal Encyclical, *Apostolicae Curae*, 1896.

6. I have given a disproportionate amount of space to these biblical passages because of widespread misunderstandings. See R. T. France, *Women in the Church's Ministry – A Test-Case for Biblical Hermeneutics*.

Chapter 7   Working Together

1. Kenneth Grubb, A *Layman Looks at the Church*, pp. 161, 112.

2. *The Lambeth Conference*, 1958, p.1.26.

3. The story is again found in Deuteronomy 1. 9-18

Chapter 8   Choosing Leaders

1. Concerning vocation, see Steve Walton, A *Call to Live – Vocation for Everyone*.

2. See *The Care of Candidates – Before and After Selection Conferences*

Chapter 9   Frailty and Renewal

1. *Under Authority – Report on Clergy Discipline*.

2. See Gordon MacDonald, *Ordering Your Private World*.

3. See Gaius Davies, *Stress – The Challenge to Christian Caring*; Mary Anne Coates, *Clergy Stress*; Andrew Irvine, *Between Two Worlds*.

4. See Gordon W. Kuhrt, *Clergy Security – a discussion paper* (available from the Ministry Division, Church House, Westminster).

5. House of Bishops, *Issues in Human Sexuality*.

6. See the paper *Clergy Security* for more detail and recommendations.

Select Bibliography

Advisory Board of Ministry of the Church of England, *Regulations for Non-Stipendiary Ministry*, ABM Policy Paper No. 5, 1994

Advisory Board of Ministry of the Church of England, *Stranger in the Wings*, A Report on Local Non-Stipendiary Ministry, ABM Policy Paper No. 8, Church House Publishing, 1998

Advisory Board of Ministry of the Church of England, *Shaping Ministry for a Missionary Church – A Review of Diocesan Ministry Strategy Documents*, ABM Ministry Paper No. 18, 1998

Advisory Board of Ministry of the Church of England, *The Care of Candidates Before and After Selection Conferences*, ABM Ministry Paper No. 16, 1997

Archbishops' Group on the Episcopate, Report of *Episcopal Ministry*, Church House Publishing, 1990

Peter Baelz and William Jacob (eds), *Ministers of the Kingdom – Exploration in Non-Stipendiary Ministry*, CIO, 1985

Board of Education of the Church of England, *All Are Called –Towards a Theology of the Laity*, Church House Publishing, 1985

Board of Education of the Church of England, *Called to New Life –The World of Discipleship*, Church House Publishing, 1999

Michael Bowering (ed.), *Priesthood Here and Now*, Diocese of Newcastle, 1994

Colin Buchanan, *Is the Church of England Biblical? An Anglican Ecclesiology*, Darton, Longman and Todd, 1988

Mary Ann Coates, *Clergy Stress*, SPCK, 1989

John N. Collins, *Diakonia – Reinterpreting the Ancient Sources*, Oxford University Press, 1990

Steven Croft, *Ministry in Three Dimensions – Ordination and Leadership in the Local Church*, Darton, Longman and Todd, 1999

Gaius Davies, *Stress – The Challenge to Christian Caring*, Kingsway, 1988

Avery Dulles, *Models of the Church*, Gill and Macmillan, second ed., 1988

R. T. France, *Women in the Church's Ministry – A Test-Case for Biblical Hermeneutics*, Paternoster, 1995

J. M. Francis, and L. F. Francis (eds), *Tentmaking — Perspectives on Self-Supporting Ministry*, Gracewing, 1998

John Fuller, and Patrick Vaughan, (eds), *Working for the Kingdom — The Story of Ministers in Secular Employment*, SPCK, 1986

General Synod of the Church of England, *Under Authority — Report on Clergy Discipline*, Church House Publishing, 1996

Michael Green, *Freed to Serve*, Hodder and Stoughton, third ed. 1996 (first ed. 1983)

Kenneth Grubb, *A Layman Looks at the Church*, Hodder and Stoughton, 1964

Christine Hall (ed.), *The Deacon's Ministry*, Gracewing ,1992

Christine Hall and Robert Hannaford (eds), *Order and Ministry*, Gracewing, 1996

Rhoda Hiscox, *Celebrating Reader Ministry*, Mowbray, 1991

Mark Hodge, *Non-Stipendiary Ministry in the Church of England*, CIO, 1983

House of Bishops of the Church of England, *The Ordination of Women to the Priesthood* — A Second Report by the House of Bishops, Church House Publishing, 1988

House of Bishops of the Church of England, *The Ordination of Women to the Priesthood* — A *Digest*, Church House Publishing,1990

House of Bishops of the Church of England, *Issues in Human Sexuality*, Church House Publishing, 1991

House of Bishops of the Church of England, *Eucharistic Presidency*, A Theological Statement by the House of Bishops, Church House Publishing, 1997

House of Bishops of the Church of England, *Good News People — Recognizing Diocesan Evangelists*, Church House Publishing, 1999

James B. Hurley, *Man and Woman in Biblical Perspective*, IVP, 1981

Andrew Irvine, *Between Two Worlds*, Mowbray, 1997

Philip King, *Good News for a Suffering World*, Monarch, 1996

T. G. King, *Readers: A Pioneer Ministry*, Central Readers' Board, 1973

Gordon Kuhrt, *Believing in Baptism*, Mowbray, 1987

Gordon Kuhrt, *Clergy Security — A Discussion Paper*, The Ministry Division of the Church of England, 1998

Select Bibliography

Lambeth Conference, *Report of the Lambeth Conference* 1958, SPCK, 1958

Giles Legood (ed.), *Chaplaincy – The Church's Sector Ministries*, Cassell, 1999

Gordon MacDonald, *Ordering Your Private World*, Highland, 1984

Alwyn Marriage, *The People of God – A Royal Priesthood*, Darton, Longman and Todd, 1995

Robert Martineau, *The Office and Work of a Reader*, Mowbray, 1980

Ministry Division of the Church of England, *Statistics of Licensed Ministers*, Annual

Mission and Unity, Board of, (Church of England), *Priesthood of the Ordained Ministry*, BMU, 1986

R. C. Moberly, *Ministerial Priesthood*, Murray, 1907 (first ed. 1897)

Rosie Nixson, *Liberating Women for the Gospel*, Hodder and Stoughton, 1997

Nigel Peyton, *Dual-Role Ministry*, Grove Pastoral Booklet, 1998

Portsmouth, Bishop of (ed.), *Deacons in the Ministry of the Church*, Church House Publishing, 1988

Michael Ramsey, *The Christian Priest Today*, SPCK, 1972, (rev.ed.) 1985

Alistair Redfern, *Ministry and Priesthood*, Darton, Longman and Todd, 1999

Elaine Storkey, *What's Right with Feminism?*, SPCK, 1985

Elaine Storkey and Margaret Hebblethwaite, *Conversations on Christian Feminism*, Fount, 1999

John R.W. Stott, *One People – Clergy and Laity in God's Church*, Falcon, 1969

John R.W. Stott, *I Believe in Preaching*, Hodder and Stoughton, 1982

John R.W. Stott, *The Preacher's Portrait*, Tyndale Press, 1961

Jean Tillard, *What Priesthood Has the Ministry?*, Grove Booklet on Ministry and Worship, 1973

John Tiller, *A Strategy for the Church's Ministry*, CIO, 1983

Andrew Walker, *Restoring the Kingdom*, Hodder and Stoughton (rev. ed.), 1998

Steve Walton, *A Call to Live – Vocation for Everyone*, SPCK Triangle, 1994

World Council of Churches, *One Lord, One Baptism*, Commission on Faith and Order Paper, SCM, 1961

World Council of Churches, *Baptism, Eucharist and Ministry*, Faith and Order Paper 111, Geneva, 1982

Index